Carmen

BLACK DOG OPERA LIBRARY

Carmen

GEORGES BIZET

TEXT BY DAVID FOIL

BLACK DOG
& LEVENTHAL
PUBLISHERS
NEW YORK

Published by
Black Dog & Leventhal Publishers, Inc.
151 West 19th Street
New York, NY 10011

Distributed by
Workman Publishing Company
708 Broadway
New York, NY 10003

Designed by Alleycat Design, Inc.

Series editor: Judith Dupré

Book manufactured in **Singapore**

ISBN: 1-884822-81-9

h g f e d

FOREWORD

*E*verybody knows Carmen—the great melodies from Georges Bizet's score are among the most recognized melodies in all of music. But the opera itself is a mesmerizing drama of fatal attraction—still startling in its erotic power and violent intensity, still seductive in its imagination and its potent musical personality. The version of the opera you are about to hear is exactly what the composer intended, restoring the work's original theatrical intensity, both as music and as drama.

You will hear the entire opera on the two compact discs included on the inside front and back covers of this book. As you explore the book, you will discover the story behind the opera and its creation, the background of the composer, biographies of the principal singers and conductor, and the opera's text, or libretto, both in the original French and in an English translation. Special commentary has been included throughout the libretto to aid in your appreciation and to highlight key moments in the action and the score.

Enjoy this book and enjoy the music.

Carmen

"This time I have written a work that is all clarity and vivacity, full of color and melody," the French composer Georges Bizet told a friend late in 1874, adding, "It will be entertaining. Come along—I think you are going to like it."

At that point, Bizet was genuinely pleased with the new opéra comique he had just completed, and was looking forward to its production at the Opéra-Comique in Paris. But this would probably be the last time he felt completely happy about his new creation, which was called *Carmen*. The rehearsals would be difficult and frustrating; the premiere on March 3, 1875, would be met with apathy. Bizet, who knew he was on to something new in *Carmen*, was bitterly disappointed by this response. Sadly, he did not live to see his work prove a

Left POSTER OF EMMA CALVE, A FAMOUS EARLY CARMEN, CIRCA 1910.
Above GEORGES BIZET

PROSPER MÉRIMÉE

triumphant success only a few years later. He was taken seriously ill shortly after the premiere of *Carmen* and died exactly three months later, early on the morning of June 3, 1875, after the Opéra-Comique gave its thirty-third performance of the opera. Bizet was thirty-six years old.

Carmen has retained more of its allure, magic, and sheer theatrical intensity than almost any other opera in the mainstream repertoire, despite a century of disregard for Bizet's original intentions and a broad popularity that constantly threatens to dump the whole enterprise into the questionable realm of camp. Bizet and his librettists Henri Meilhac and Ludovic Halévy based their work on a dark novella by the French writer Prosper Mérimée. In Mérimée's story, a psychotic soldier, Don José, recounts his obsessive love for an irresistibly carnal creature named Carmen, an obsession that ends with his killing her. In the opera, the bleakness of Mérimée's novella is mitigated somewhat, but the subtle background detail seems to have had a powerful impact on Bizet's music. Making an opera of *Carmen* was apparently his idea and, though he does not have a reputation as a true innovator, he found an uncanny way to reach the bourgeois audience for which he was writing while remaining true to the primal intensity of the material.

Indeed, Georges Bizet's reputation as one of France's greatest composers of the nineteenth century rests almost entirely on *Carmen*. Few composers have shown as much promise as Bizet did as a young man. He was encouraged from an early age by his parents, both of whom were musicians, and entered the Paris Conservatory at the age of nine. As a teenager, he took prizes there in piano and organ performance, and in fugue writing; at the age of nineteen, he was awarded the prestigious Prix de Rome, the seal of approval from the French musical establishment to a young composer. However, Bizet had little interest in writing the kind of music the establishment expected—masses, cantatas, grand symphonic works—and he ran into trouble by trying to write an opera as part of his obligation as the Prix de Rome laureate. (The lighthearted work in question, entitled *Don Procopio*, would not be performed until 1906.) In fact, trouble plagued all of Bizet's many efforts at writing opera. The only other Bizet opera performed today, *Les Pêcheurs de perles* (The Pearl Fishers), completed in 1863, is best known for containing two beautiful arias and a hugely popular duet ("Au fond du temple saint" for tenor and baritone) in an attractive but less than extraordinary score set in an exotic location to a turgid libretto.

The idea of setting *Carmen* as an opera seems to have occurred to Bizet around 1873. His librettists Halévy and Meilhac were a highly esteemed partnership in French opera who wrote, either together or with other collaborators, the librettos for operas by Clement Delibes, Friedrich Flotow, and Jules Massenet and most of Jacques Offenbach's operettas, as well as the plays that inspired the Viennese operettas *Die Fledermaus* and *The Merry Widow*. It seems neither Halévy nor Meilhac—who were consumed with projects they considered

AN 1878 ILLUSTRATION OF CARMEN'S FINAL SCENE.

more important—thought much of the project or the libretto they fashioned for *Carmen*, and Bizet himself tinkered with the text to bring it to the point where it met his specific demands for the musical score and the drama. The result is a libretto as fine as any in the history of opera, setting the stage for the composition of a score that now seems astonishingly bold.

Bizet's music prior to *Carmen* was unfailingly skillful, attractive, and very much influenced by the work of the respected French composer Charles Gounod, who was his mentor. In his earlier works, Bizet showed a fine gift for melody and an evolving interest in the colors and effects that could be drawn from an orchestra. Yet little of this prepares us for the volatile beauty of the *Carmen* score. The very year he began writing *Carmen*, Bizet had been working on *Don Rodrigue,* a five-act grand opera about the hero of Spanish history known as El Cid. He abandoned the project because the Opéra burned, temporarily ceasing production and thus eliminating the possibility of a performance; his friend Ernest Guiraud later intimated that the disappearance of the score was a great loss to music. When parts of the *Don Rodrigue* score resurfaced decades later, they revealed another competent but uninspired effort, with little of the genius of *Carmen*, despite a shared Spanish setting.

It is clear that Bizet was both inspired and liberated by the story of *Carmen*, resulting in a score that is surprisingly deft, a quality that heightens the work's ambiguous sensuality and mood. Nothing illustrates this lightness of touch more than the breathtaking signature melody that ignites the opera's prelude. Where did this melody come from? It sounds like nothing else in music. Yes, it

suggests Spain and a festive scene, but has something else—a wide-eyed, come-what-may excitement, a shocking virility, and a primal intensity that hints at what Carmen instinctively knows and what Don José is afraid to acknowledge. The detail in Bizet's musical plan is extraordinary. Even though one of the score's most famous passages, the habanera sung by Carmen, relies on the melody of the song "El arreglito" by the Spanish songwriter Sebastián de Yradier, Bizet (who thought it was a folk tune) tweaked the rhythm and shape of the melody in a manner that utterly transformed it. The crowning glory of *Carmen* is the final duet, in which the crazed Don José confronts Carmen in a dazzlingly compact fourth act that lasts barely twenty minutes. After the crowd departs for the bullfight, Bizet draws us into the vortex by echoing the signature theme and dragging it down, down, down chromatically, preparing us for what is about to happen. The duet itself is an exquisitely beautiful showpiece for the two singers, heartbreaking in its inevitability and magical in its streamlined eloquence. No less an orchestral master than Richard Strauss once said, "If you want to know how to orchestrate . . . study the score of *Carmen*. What wonderful economy, and how every note and rest is in its proper place."

Why, then, did audiences and critics scratch their heads and recoil when they first heard *Carmen*? Why did Bizet's score confound and infuriate the orchestra that was to play it for the first time? Some of the singers were puzzled, too. The ladies of the chorus, in particular, resented the fact that they were expected to smoke cigarettes and fight onstage (some of them were taken ill in the process), and there was general uneasiness about the sexual candor of the story. However, Bizet's leading singers supported him and threatened to walk out in protest if any kind of censorship was attempted. There is no evidence to

ROSA PONSELLE AS CARMEN.

THE CIGARETTE GIRLS IN FRONT OF A WALL COVERED WITH GRAFFITI IN A SET DESIGNED IN 1981 FOR THE SAN FRANCISCO OPERA BY JEAN-PIERRE PONNELLE.

support speculation that Bizet was forced against his will to make extensive last-minute cuts and changes in the score. The morning of the premiere of *Carmen*, in fact, the composer was made a chevalier of the Legion of Honor. At last success seemed to be imminent.

It was not to be. Contrary to legend, *Carmen* was not a failure at its premiere, and it did not directly bring about Bizet's death three months later. It can best be described as being neither a flop nor a hit. At the premiere, Bizet reportedly told the young composer Vincent d'Indy, who came to congratulate him and found him pacing outside near the stage door, "I sense defeat. I foresee a definite and hopeless flop. This time I am really sunk." The audience's unenthusiastic, not to say perplexed, response and the negative reviews only reinforced his fears. His mentor Gounod gracelessly insisted that Bizet had stolen the melody for Micaëla's third-act aria from him, and what hadn't been stolen from him and others was mere "sauce without the fish." Opening-night reviews berated Bizet for the lack of color in his score and—worst of all, to these critics—for a tendency toward Wagnerian techniques. In the wake of the Franco-Prussian war, any suggestion of Richard Wagner's influence was considered in certain quarters to be an insult to French art. "Fed on the enharmonic succulences of the prophets of the music of the future, Bizet seems to have fed his soul on this diet, thereby killing it," one critic wrote, warming up to continue, "Ingenious details in the orchestra, daring dissonances, and instrumental subtleties cannot portray the uterine agonies of Mademoiselle Carmen and the wishes of her wayward lovers . . . the music lacks novelty and distinction. There is no plan, no unity in its style . . . it is neither dramatic nor scenic."

The chief prophet of the "music of the future," Wagner in fact abhorred *Carmen*. So intense was his dislike that it widened a long-standing breach between him and the philosopher Friedrich Nietzsche that would never heal. Nietzsche found *Carmen* to be a transcendent work of art because the score manages to be "wicked, subtle, and fatalistic" while remaining accessible. "What is good is easy," Nietzsche wrote as his first aesthetic law, "everything divine runs with light feet." The Russian composer Pyotr Ilich Tchaikovsky was an early fan of *Carmen*, too, and insisted that it would soon enjoy world-wide popularity.

No one would dispute the fact that *Carmen* is a masterpiece, and no one has seriously since its apathetic premiere. Yet the "real" *Carmen* has proved elusive for more than the century that it has been in the repertoire of opera houses all over the world. *Carmen* is not an opera, in the strict grand opera sense of the word, but an opéra-comique. *Opéra-comique* is a French term that has no fixed meaning—not all the works so labeled fit the contemporary understanding of comedy—but it has come to refer to an operatic work with comic elements that also has spoken dialogue. In Paris in the midnineteenth century that dialogue distinguished comic opera from the sober, overstuffed grand operas so popular at the Opéra. The theater known as the Opéra-Comique was an altogether less pretentious place than the Opéra, drawing a more bourgeois crowd, and it provided a more relaxed atmosphere for operatic entertainment.

By the early 1870s, Bizet had had no success in writing a grand opera that interested the public, and he decided shortly before he set to work on *Carmen* that he should leave that task to others. He wrote *Carmen* for the Opéra-Comique, certain he had found a level on which to communicate with an audience. He crafted a score with a prelude and twenty-seven musical numbers to be linked by spoken dialogue. He personally corrected the proofs on the published score in this form which was published by the Choudens firm in 1875. Yet, for almost a hundred years, the Choudens score was almost never performed.

Much of *Carmen's* popularity rests on an adaptation of the score by Ernest Guiraud, the gifted New Orleans–born, Paris–based composer who was one of Bizet's best friends. Guiraud created this new version for the Vienna premiere of *Carmen* in October of 1875, replacing Bizet, who had signed the contract to write the recitatives for the production the day before he died. Guiraud made the score more appealing for the opera house by composing sung recitatives to replace the spoken dialogue, as Bizet himself had been contracted to do. There were some compelling reasons for this change. First of all, the absence of dialogue and the presence of sung recitative made *Carmen* sound more like a grand opera. Second, making it an opera that was fully sung made the performance easier for singers who at the time resented the amount of additional acting they were required to do. Third, opera in the late nineteenth century was not always performed in the language in which it was written, and the distinctively French opéra-comique—with its pointillistic interplay of the French language both spoken and sung—lost a great deal in translation. But as Guiraud made *Carmen* a more accessible repertory piece and created the version most audiences know,

he blunted the razor-sharp double-edged nature of the true opéra-comique Bizet had envisioned.

Carmen is not a pretty story, despite the image of lusty gypsy women with cascades of hair and roses tucked behind their ears that is traditionally associated with the opera. The title character is a woman who is irresistible to men, with a kind of wild dignity all her own. She does whatever she feels like doing, until she makes the fatal mistake of ruining the life of the deeply disturbed Don José. She chooses to live in a world that tolerates her, a world of

MARILYN HORNE IN THE TITLE ROLE.

GERALDINE FARRAR AS CARMEN.

deception, thievery, cruelty, and violence. Violence is the flip side of beauty in Bizet's opera—in the text, in the action, and in the music itself—and the cruelty of the actions of everyone involved (except Don José's selfless fiancée Micaëla) is stunning. Slightly later, Italians would claim *Carmen* as the forerunner of verismo opera, a vividly realistic style of opera that flourished in Italy around the turn of the twentieth century. *Cavalleria rusticana* and *I pagliacci* are examples

JOSE CARRERAS AS THE
PSYCHOTIC DON JOSÉ.

of the verismo style and, ultimately, not unlike *Carmen* in their murderous intensity.

But remember Bizet's description: "all clarity and vivacity . . . It will be entertaining." If the Italians thought *Carmen* prefigured *I pagliacci,* it was probably because they knew *Carmen* from the Guiraud version, where elements of comedy and Bizet's strikingly ambiguous atmosphere had virtually been eliminated. As in a classic American musical comedy, the dialogue between musical numbers in an opéra-comique tends to underscore the characters' humanity, to reveal subtleties and interesting contradictions in their personalities. Instead of the alluring, vampish prima donna that reigns supreme in Guiraud's version, the Carmen of Bizet's opéra-comique is raunchy, sometimes wickedly funny, petty, tantalizingly remote, and unpredictable. Likewise, Bizet's Don José is not the bellowing overgrown boy he can sometimes seem in the Guiraud version, but a deeply conflicted young man full of repressed rage. He is teetering on the brink of insanity, an obsessive-compulsive who becomes a homicidal stalker. In the case of Don José, the opéra-comique version does not make the character lighter but much, much darker.

For all the criticism of Guiraud's version of *Carmen*, it must be said that the quality of his work was excellent. The recitatives are so effective musically that it is sometimes difficult to know what was written by Bizet and what was written by Guiraud. Its effectiveness made it the accepted version, to such an extent that curiosity about the opéra-comique version was left to scholars. However, in 1964, a musicologist named Fritz Oeser discovered—in a dust-covered, forgotten cupboard at the Opéra-Comique —a conductor's score and orchestral parts that allowed him to reconstruct elements of the score Bizet had not included in the edition published by Choudens in 1875. Oeser's discoveries are fascinating, though Bizet scholar Winton Dean makes a compelling case for viewing the 1875 Choudens score without the Guiraud recitatives as the most authoritative one. If Oeser's new edition raised a controversy, it did reintroduce the idea of presenting *Carmen* in its original form, which is now accepted as the ideal in recordings and in the world's

GLADYS SWARTHOUT
AS CARMEN.

major opera houses. Many recordings of *Carmen* since Oeser's discovery have borrowed from Oeser's edition. But this recording, made in 1969–70, led the way in restoring the primacy of Bizet's 1875 Choudens score. At long last, this is the opera—or rather the opéra-comique—that Bizet meant for the world to hear.

The Story of Carmen

ACT I

It is a typical, sleepy day in Seville. Soldiers linger in the square outside the armory, next to a cigarette factory, as the townspeople go about their business. So little is happening that, for the soldiers, the highlight of the guards' watch is the appearance of a shy country girl from Navarre named Micaëla. She is looking for Don José. The corporal Moralès tells her that Don José is due shortly with the relief guard and invites her to wait in the guardhouse. Micaëla recoils, taken aback by the laughing soldiers' interest, and tells Moralès she will return later. Don José arrives with the change of guard and learns of Micaëla's visit.

Zuniga, the lieutenant, kids Don José about his country girlfriend and then asks him what he knows about the cigarette factory girls. Don José insists he pays no attention to them. At that moment, a ringing bell signals a smoking break for the factory girls, which attracts a crowd of young men hoping to catch their attention. The girls enjoy the ritual but, in truth, the men are interested in only one girl—the mysterious and alluring Carmen. Carmen is unfazed by their attention, as they beg her to choose one of them as her lover. She answers to the rhythms of the habanera: love is as untamable as a wild bird, as prone to wandering as a gypsy. Her indifference only intensifies the men's interest.

Carmen tosses an acacia flower to the one man in the square who pays no attention to her—Don José, who is repelled by her boldness yet immediately

A SCENE FROM ACT I IN A PRODUCTION AT THE HOUSTON GRAND OPERA.

drawn into her spell. He keeps the flower and quickly hides it in his tunic when Micaëla suddenly appears. She brings Don José a letter and some money from his mother, as well as a kiss; they reminisce about their happiness at home. In the letter, Don José's mother begs him to marry Micaëla and, when his tour of duty ends, return to live near her. Embarrassed by the suggestion, Micaëla leaves, saying they will meet again shortly.

At that moment, a fight breaks out in the cigarette factory. Zuniga, surrounded by screaming girls trying to tell him who started it, sends Don José inside to break it up. Don José emerges with a defiant Carmen, who has slashed the face of another girl. She barely offers a defense of her behavior and, when pressed, only sings derisively in Zuniga's face. He leaves to obtain a warrant for her arrest, charging Don José to guard Carmen. She tricks Don José into a conversation and begins to tease him with the prospect of spending an evening (and more) with her at the tavern of Lillas Pastia, on the outskirts of Seville. He is unnerved by her attention and eventually agrees to untie her

PLACIDO DOMINGO AS DON JOSÉ.

hands so she can escape. When Zuniga returns, Carmen is led away and then suddenly pushes Don José to the ground, humiliating him as she runs away laughing, her friends thwarting the soldiers' attempts to recapture her. The lieutenant angrily orders a stunned Don José to be arrested and led away to the brig.

ACT II

Carmen is holding court at Lillas Pastia's with her gypsy friends Frasquita and Mercédès. They sing and dance to the great enjoyment of the soldiers who are pursuing them, led by none other than Zuniga. Carmen is cool to Zuniga, who thinks she is angry at him for trying to have her arrested. She is actually piqued that he had Don José thrown into prison, and she is delighted to hear that the unfortunate soldier is being released that night. They are interrupted by the arrival of Escamillo, the great toreador of Granada, who raises the roof of Lillas Pastia's with a toast after Zuniga buys him a drink. Escamillo is immediately drawn to Carmen, who teases and strings him along with her indifference. Zuniga and his men leave with Escamillo, who tells Carmen he will return for her.

Once the crowd has left, a nervous Lillas Pastia tells Frasquita that the smugglers Dancaïro and Remendado have returned. The gypsy women are delighted, however, and learn that the smugglers need their help in bringing in contraband from Gibraltar. All agree that women are indispensable in such an enterprise, though Carmen surprises them by saying she will not join them. She is, she says, in love. They laugh at her, but she insists that she is only interested in waiting for Don José's release from prison.

SOLANGE MICHEL (B. 1912) AS CARMEN.

When they hear Don José's voice in the distance, Dancaïro suggests Carmen enlist his aid and have him run away with them. She says she will try, as she hustles the smugglers out of the tavern in order to offer a proper greeting to the young soldier. He becomes jealous when Carmen tells him that Zuniga has been pursuing her. She then calms him by dancing for his enjoyment, accompanied by her castanets. As she dances, he hears a bugle call in the distance, summoning the troops back to the barracks. Don José tells her suddenly he must leave. Carmen explodes in rage, ridiculing his passion and his sense of duty, while berating herself for wasting her time on him.

Don José silences her by producing the acacia flower she tossed him in their first encounter. With a feverish intensity, he tells her that the flower has been his emblem of hope during his imprisonment—proof of his passionate love for her. Carmen sees her opportunity, scoffing at his assurances and insisting that if he really loved her, he would join her and her friends in their new enterprise. Don José is initially seduced by the idea, then recoils at the thought of being a deserter. He prepares to leave, telling her again how much he loves her, when Zuniga enters to confront him. A hysterical Don José

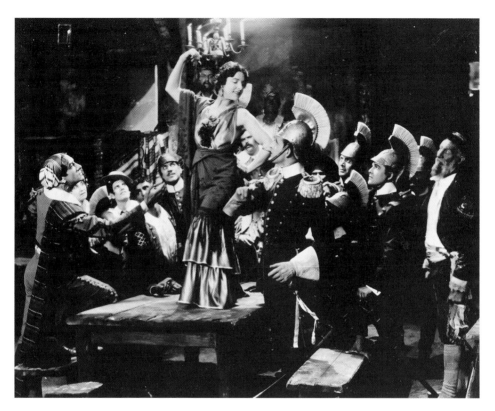

CARMEN (GERALDINE FARRAR) DANCES FOR DON JOSÉ.

draws his sword on Zuniga. Carmen calls for help from Dancaïro and Remendado. They enter with the other gypsies and tell Zuniga that his timing has been unfortunate. When Carmen again asks Don José to join them, he realizes he now has no choice, and she assures him he will come to love the carefree life of the gypsy.

FRASQUITA (GLORIA LIND, LEFT) AND MERCEDES (HELEN VANNI)
READ THE TAROT DECK.

ACT III

Months later, the band of smugglers is still hauling contraband over the mountains. They pause to rest, as Dancaïro and Remendado go ahead to find out how to slip unnoticed into the next town. Don José, who is clearly miserable, tells Carmen that his mother lives nearby. The charm of their relationship has worn off for Carmen, and she suggests he return home. He flies into a rage at the idea. As a diversion, Frasquita and Mercédès bring out the tarot cards to read their fortunes. The wisdom of the cards amuses them but Carmen is shocked by what they reveal for herself and Don José—death. Believing what the cards tell her, Carmen knows now what lies in store.

Dancaïro and Remendado return, saying they need the women's help in distracting some customs guards. The increasingly despondent Don José is left to guard the loot. A guide appears with Micaëla who is searching for Don José. She tells the guide she will proceed alone without fear. Once she is alone, she gives voice to her fears and prays to God for strength. When Micaëla finally sees Don José, she so startles him that he fires his gun without seeing her.

At that moment, with Micaëla cowering unseen, Escamillo enters and tells Don José that the shot just missed him. After introducing himself, he informs

SCENE FROM A 1990 PRODUCTION OF CARMEN AT THE LYRIC OPERA OF CHICAGO.

Don José that he is looking for Carmen, with whom he is in love. Don José becomes furious and challenges Escamillo to a knife fight. Escamillo, the superior fighter, humors him but then stumbles and suddenly is at Don José's mercy. Only the arrival of Carmen and the other gypsies saves him. Escamillo laughs at the delicious irony of his salvation and invites Carmen and her friends to be his guests at the bullfight in Seville.

Don José, already beside himself, is stunned when the smugglers find Micaëla hiding in the rocks; she tells him that his mother is calling for him. Carmen tells him to go and, though he resists leaving her to Escamillo's favors, he leaves with Micaëla once he learns that his mother is dying and wants to see him one last time. Don José warns Carmen that their affair is not over. Once he leaves, Carmen's fancy turns to the distant sound of Escamillo's singing.

ACT IV

Outside the arena in Seville, excitement is growing in anticipation of the great bullfight that will feature Escamillo. A huge crowd awaits the ceremonial procession to the bullring, culminating in the arrival of Escamillo in his toreador regalia, with a resplendent Carmen on his arm. Frasquita and Mercédès have learned that Don José—who is now pursued by the army as a deserter—might be in the vicinity. Before entering the arena in the wake of Escamillo's procession, they try to warn Carmen who dismisses their concern and sends them on into the arena. Alone in the square, she awaits her destiny. Don José emerges from the shadows to tell her that he has not come to harm her, and pleads with her to accept the inevitability of their love. Carmen refuses, and tells him that they are

THE TOREADOR PROCESSION.

finished. He does not believe her, begging her to take him back. Carmen, distracted by the crowd's cheers for Escamillo, tries to make her way to the bullring but is blocked by Don José who demands to know if she and Escamillo are lovers. Carmen answers that she and the toreador are indeed lovers and that not even the threat of death can make her deny it. The full weight of Carmen's contempt finally hits Don José. She further insults him by hurling the ring he had given her in his face. Shattered, his ears ringing with the cheers of Escamillo's admirers, Don José attacks Carmen, stabbing her to death. He collapses over her body, admitting his guilt as he professes his love for her.

CARMEN MEETS HER DESTINY IN A 1972 PRODUCTION AT THE METROPOLITAN OPERA.

The Performers

GRACE BUMBRY (Carmen) has had a remarkable career as a mezzo-soprano, with occasional forays into the soprano repertory. Born in 1937 in St. Louis, she began singing in church choirs as a little girl and began attending Northwestern University in 1955 as a student of Lotte Lehmann. Bumbry followed Lehmann to the Music Academy of the West in Santa Barbara, California, to continue the study that would shape her as a singer. Her professional debut came in a concert performance in London in 1959; her operatic debut a year later, where she stunned audiences at the Paris Opéra as a last-minute substitute in the role of Amneris in *Aida*. The fact that she was African-American added to the glamour of the debut, and it created a positive furor when Wieland Wagner subsequently signed her to sing the role of Venus in Wagner's *Tannhäuser* at the 1961 Bayreuth Festival. The triumph Bumbry enjoyed there made her an instant celebrity. Her return to the United States brought her to the Kennedy White House and an important concert tour. Her debut at the Chicago Lyric Opera in 1963 repeated

GRACE BUMBRY AS CARMEN.

her Bayreuth success as Venus, and her Metropolitan Opera debut was made two years later as Princess Eboli in Verdi's *Don Carlo*. Bumbry's Carmen created a sensation at the 1966 Salzburg Festival under Herbert von Karajan (a production that was filmed), and it became one of her trademark roles. In the early 1970s, Bumbry took advantage of her remarkable range and began singing soprano roles. The title role in Strauss's *Salome* became a particular favorite, as did the fearsome role of Abigaille in Verdi's *Nabucco,* but she also had great success in the title roles of *Tosca* and *Aida.* (She also continued to sing the mezzo-soprano role of Amneris, just as she began to sing Elisabeth as well as Venus in *Tannhäuser.*) Bumbry also sang Bess in the first Metropolitan Opera production of Gershwin's *Porgy and Bess.* In the 1980s, she returned to the great mezzo-soprano roles upon which her reputation rested. Her voice was always remarkable for its expressive richness, power, and extensive range—qualities largely undiminished when she returned to the Metropolitan Opera for a gala appearance in 1996.

JON VICKERS (Don José) exemplified the art of the dramatic tenor throughout his long and remarkable career. Born in 1926 in Prince Albert, Saskatchewan, he emerged from unlikely beginnings in provincial Canada—where he managed F.W. Woolworth stores and served as a purchasing agent for the Hudson Bay Company—to study voice as a scholarship student at the Royal Conservatory of Music in Toronto. Vickers made his professional operatic debut in 1952 as the Duke in *Rigoletto* at the Toronto Opera Festival, and his tremendous promise began to pay off quickly. Within five years, he was singing in London with the Royal Opera, Covent Garden, where he enjoyed great acclaim in 1958 in the title role in Luchino Visconti's legendary production there of Verdi's *Don Carlo.* The heroic profile and unique intensity of Vickers's singing made him a natural candidate for the heldentenor roles in Wagner's music-dramas. Vickers trod carefully around this potentially dangerous repertoire, sticking primarily (and with great success) with Siegmund in *Die Walküre,* the title role in *Parsifal* and, for a few years, Tristan in *Tristan und Isolde.* He sang Siegmund at the Bayreuth Festival in 1958 and recorded the role twice but avoided the heavier role of Siegfried.

Vickers's repertoire was fascinating in its breadth, and it reflected his highly personal, unusually principled approach to his career. He has had little patience with the superficial glamor and politics of the international operatic scene and has been outspoken in his disdain for those who take for granted the moral dimension of art and of being an artist. If these qualities made him a demanding colleague, they also made him an extraordinary one—Vickers delivered as a performer with astonishing consistency and tremendous dramatic power. Earlier in his career, he sang Jason in Luigi Cherubini's *Medea* opposite Maria

JON VICKERS AS DON JOSÉ AND MIRELLA FRENI AS MICAËLA IN A 1968–69 PRODUCTION AT THE METROPOLITAN OPERA.

Callas in thrilling performances with the Dallas Opera that were captured live on tape. His signature roles included Enée in Hector Berlioz's *Les Troyens* (a long-neglected opera he helped popularize), Canio in Ruggero Leoncavallo's *I pagliacci,* Florestan in Beethoven's *Fidelio* and—perhaps most unforgettably—the anguished title characters in Giuseppe Verdi's *Otello* and Benjamin Britten's *Peter Grimes.*

MIRELLA FRENI (Micaëla) was born in 1935 in Modena, a few months earlier than the city's most famous son, Luciano Pavarotti. As infants, the two singers-to-be—who would later become affectionate colleagues—shared the same wet nurse, and their mothers worked in the same cigarette factory. Freni began studying voice with her uncle, making her first public appearance at the age of eleven with another prodigy, the pianist Leone Magiera, who would become her first husband. She made her opera debut in 1955 in Modena as Micaëla in *Carmen*, inaugurating what would be a stellar international stage and recording career of extraordinary range and longevity. After singing several seasons with provincial Italian houses, Freni made strong impressions in debuts with the Amsterdam Opera (1959), London's Covent Garden (1961), and Milan's La Scala (1962), quickly becoming one of Europe's most sought-after lyric sopranos. The role of Mimì in *La Bohème* became her calling card, especially after her performance in the successful 1963 film of Franco Zeffirelli's La Scala production, conducted by Herbert von Karajan. Freni sang Mimì in her debuts at Moscow's Bolshoi Opera (1964) and New York's Metropolitan Opera (1965). She also excelled in such roles as Susanna in *Le nozze di Figaro,* Violetta in *La traviata,* Zerlina in *Don Giovanni,* Marguerite in *Faust,* and Juliette in *Roméo et Juliette.* In the 1970s, when Freni decided to sing heavier roles—a dangerous choice for a lyric soprano—many critics predicted that it would ruin her voice. Bolstered by a steady technique and the sensitive support of conductors such as von Karajan and Riccardo Muti, she was instead acclaimed for bringing a distinctive lyrical warmth to performances and recordings of the title role in *Aida,* Cio-Cio-San in *Madama Butterfly,* Elisabetta in *Don Carlo,* and Leonora in *La forza del destino.* In 1981, she married the Bulgarian bass Nicolai Ghiaurov, a colleague who virtually became her professional partner, notably after Freni began singing

Russian roles such as Tatyana in *Eugene Onegin.* In the 1990s, she has been noted for her performances in the demanding prima donna roles of such verismo warhorses as *Adriana Lecouvreur* and *Fedora.*

KOSTAS PASKALIS (Escamillo) began his career with a seven-year stint in the ensemble of the Athens Opera, where he made his professional debut in 1951 in the title role of *Rigoletto* after studying at the Athens Conservatory. Born in 1929 in Lebadea, Greece, he enjoyed a successful debut at the Vienna Staatsoper in 1958, leading to an international career that would last for the next quarter-century. The dramatic intensity of Paskalis's singing was a fine match for the signature baritone roles in the Italian repertoire. He sang frequently at the Vienna Staatsoper and with Berlin's Deutsche Oper, London's Royal Opera at Covent Garden and, in Russia during the Soviet era, with the Bolshoi and Kirov companies. His Metropolitan Opera debut came in 1965 in the role of Carlo in *La forza del destino.* He also sang with other American companies; in 1979, he was reunited with tenor Jon Vickers in a production of Verdi's *Otello* at the Houston Grand Opera. Because Paskalis came to prominence at a time when the baritones Robert Merrill, Tito Gobbi, Ettore Bastianini, Piero Cappuccilli, and Sherrill Milnes were singing, he did not record as frequently as they did. Yet he was an outstanding singer who had particular success with the challenging role of Escamillo in *Carmen,* which he sang (also with Grace Bumbry and Jon Vickers) in Herbert von Karajan's film of his Salzburg Festival production.

RAFAEL FRÜHBECK DE BURGOS (born Rafael Frühbeck) is the son of a German father and a Spanish mother whose training and repertoire are largely reflective of that heritage. Born in the Spanish town of Burgos in 1933, he began his studies as a violinist at the conservatory in Bilbao in 1950. From 1956 until 1958, he studied conducting with Kurt Eichhorn at Munich's Hochschule für Musik, after which he returned to Bilbao to conduct the city's municipal orchestra. Frühbeck de Burgos quickly emerged as Spain's most promising conductor and, in 1962, was named principal conductor of Madrid's Orquesta Nacional de España, a post he held for fifteen years. He simultaneously served as general-musikdirektor of the Düsseldorf Symphony Orchestra (1966–71) and, for two years, as music director of the Montreal Symphony Orchestra (1975–76). In the United States, Frühbeck de Burgos has had a long association with Washington's National Symphony Orchestra, beginning with a stint as principal guest conductor in 1980. He is a frequent guest with orchestras throughout Europe and the United States. His most recent posts have included music director of Tokyo's Yomiuri Nippon Symphony Orchestra and, beginning in 1990, chief conductor of the Vienna Symphony Orchestra. Though he conducts and records the standard orchestral repertoire, he has been especially admired in Spanish music and that with a Spanish flavor, making him an obvious choice for a recording of *Carmen*.

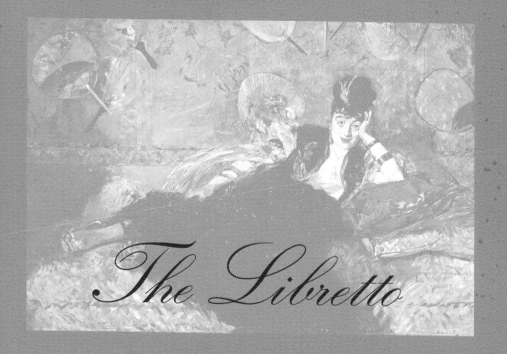

The Libretto

Act 1

disk no. 1/track 1   *Prelude*   Wild and indefinable, the thrilling melody that begins the opera's prelude becomes a symbol of the title character. It is heard again only once, in the chorus that greets the bullfighters in Act IV, but its vivid, dancing abandon is the very incarnation of Carmen. There is also a contrasting section that quotes the Toreador Song of Act II **(01:01)**, before the principal melody returns. After a deceptive pause, it is followed by a striking motive that will be heard repeatedly an ominous descending melody **(02:07)**, played against a shuddering orchestra, that represents the inexorable force of fate in Carmen's life. It plunges deeper and deeper as it develops, then rises and builds in tension to an almost unbearable point, where it simply and stunningly snaps—and the opera begins.

THE FACTORY SCENE IN A PRODUCTION AT THE METROPOLITAN OPERA.

Sur la place, chacun passe At the conclusion of the opening chorus, which describes a lazy midday scene in the square in Seville and introduces Micaëla, Bizet had written a pantomime, to be sung by Moralès, that he cut almost immediately. It is an amusing, charismatic moment **(05:54)**, written to satisfy an underemployed singer and charmingly done, but because it delays the action it is rarely performed. It was heard for the first time when this recording was released on LP and is included here.

Scene One

INTRODUCTION ∽ *A square in Seville. On the right, the door of a tobac-co factory. At the back, facing the audience, a bridge from one side of the stage to the other, reached from the stage by a winding staircase beyond the factory door. The bridge is open underneath. In front, a guard-house; in front of that, three steps leading to a covered passage. As the curtain rises, a file of soldiers (dragoons of Almanza) are grouped before the guard-house, smoking and looking at the passers-by in the square coming and going. The scene is full of animation.*

LES SOLDATS
Sur la place
chacun passe,
chacun vient, chacun va;
drôles de gens que ces gens-là!

SOLDIERS
On the square
everyone comes by,
everyone comes and goes;
funny sort of people these!

MORALÈS
A la porte du corps de garde,
pour tuer le temps,
on fume, on jase, l'on regarde
passer les passants.

MORALÈS
At the guard-house door,
to kill time,
we smoke, gossip, and watch
the passers-by.

LES SOLDATS ET MORALÈS
Sur la place, etc.

SOLDIERS AND MORALÈS
On the square, etc.

Micaëla enters.

MORALÈS
Regardez donc cette petite
qui semble vouloir nous parler.
Voyez, elle tourne, elle hésite.

LES SOLDATS
A son secours il faut aller!

MORALÈS *(à Micaëla)*
Que cherchez-vous, la belle?

MICAËLA
Moi, je cherche un brigadier.

MORALÈS
Je suis là, voilà!

MICAËLA
Mon brigadier à moi s'appelle
Don José . . . le connaissez-vous?

MORALÈS
Don José! Nous le connaissons tous.

MICAËLA
Vraiment! Est-il avec vous, je vous prie?

MORALÈS
Il n'est pas brigadier dans notre compagnie.

MICAËLA *(désolée)*
Alors, il n'est pas là?

MORALÈS
Non, ma charmante, il n'est pas là.

MORALÈS
Now look at this little lass
who seems to want to speak to us.
Look, she's turning round, she's hesitating.

SOLDIERS
We must go and help her!

MORALÈS *(to Micaëla)*
Whom are you looking for, pretty one?

MICAËLA
I'm looking for a corporal.

MORALÈS
Here I am, look!

MICAËLA
My corporal is called
Don José . . . do you know him?

MORALÈS
Don José? We all know him.

MICAËLA
Really! Is he with you, please?

MORALÈS
He isn't a corporal in our company.

MICAËLA *(disappointed)*
Then he isn't here?

MORALÈS
No, my charmer, he isn't here.

Mais tout à l'heure il y sera,
il y sera quand la garde montante
remplacera la garde descendante.

LES SOLDATS ET MORALÈS
Il y sera, etc.

MORALÈS
Mais en attendant qu'il vienne,
voulez-vous, la belle enfant,
voulez-vous prendre la peine
d'entrer chez nous un instant?

MICAËLA
Chez vous?

LES SOLDATS ET MORALÈS
Chez nous.

MICAËLA
Chez vous?

LES SOLDATS ET MORALÈS
Chez nous!

MICAËLA
Non pas, non pas.
Grand merci, messieurs les soldats.

MORALÈS
Entrez sans crainte, mignonne.
je vous promets qu'on aura, pour votre
chère personne,
tous les égards qu'il faudra.

MICAËLA
Je n'en doute pas; cependant

But in a few minutes he will be,
he'll be here when the new guard
comes to relieve the old guard.

SOLDIERS AND MORALÈS
He'll be here, etc.

MORALÈS
But while you wait for him to come
will you, my pretty child,
take the trouble
to step inside with us for a moment?

MICAËLA
Inside with you?

SOLDIERS AND MORALÈS
Inside with us.

MICAËLA
Inside with you?

SOLDIERS AND MORALÈS
Inside with us!

MICAËLA
No, no.
Many thanks, soldiers.

MORALÈS
Don't be afraid to come in, my dear,
I promise you we shall treat
your dear self
with every due respect.

MICAËLA
I don't doubt it; all the same

je reviendrai, c'est plus prudent.
Je reviendrai quand la garde montante
remplacera la garde descendante.

LES SOLDATS ET MORALÈS
Il faut rester car la garde montante,
va remplacer la garde descendante.

MORALÈS
Vous resterez!

MICAËLA
Non pas! non pas!

surrounding Micaëla

LES SOLDATS ET MORALÈS
Vous resterez!

MICAËLA
Non pas! Non pas! Non! Non! Non!
Au revoir, messieurs les soldats!

She escapes and runs off.

MORALÈS
L'oiseau s'envole,
on s'en console.
Reprenons notre passe-temps

SOLDATS
Sur la place
chacun passe, etc.

MORALÈS
Drôles de gens! Drôles de gens! Drôles de gens!

I'll come back, that's wiser.
I'll be back when the new guard comes to
relieve the old guard.

SOLDIERS AND MORALÈS
You must stay, because the new guard
is on its way to relieve the old guard.

MORALÈS
You'll stay!

MICAËLA
Indeed I'll not!

SOLDIERS AND MORALÈS
You'll stay!

MICAËLA
Indeed I'll not! No, no, no!
Goodbye, soldiers!

MORALÈS
The bird has flown;
we'll console ourselves.
Let's resume our pastime
and watch the folks go by.

SOLDIERS
On the square
everyone comes by, etc.

MORALÈS
Funny sort of people!

The movement of the passers-by which had stopped during the foregoing scene has now resumed with a certain animation. Among the people coming and going is an old gentleman with a young lady on his arm.... The old gentleman would like to continue his walk, but the young lady is doing all she can to detain him on the square. She seems anxious, uneasy. She looks to right and left. She is expecting someone, and this someone does not come. This pantomime must fit in very exactly with the following verse.

MORALÈS
Attention! Chut! Attention! Taisons-nous!
Voici venir un vieil époux,
Oeil soupçonneux, mine jalouse,
Il tient au bras sa jeune épouse;
L'amant sans doute n'est pas loin;
Il va sortir de quelque coin.
(avec les soldats)
L'amant sans doute n'est pas loin;
Il va sortir de quelque coin.

MORALÈS
Stand by! Sssh! Let's pipe down!
Look, here comes an old husband
with a suspicious eye and a jealous look,
he's holding on to his young wife by the
arm; no doubt the lover's not far off;
he'll pop out of some corner.
(With the soldiers)
No doubt the lover's not far off; he'll pop
out of some corner.

At this moment a young man comes quickly on to the square.

Ah! ah! ah! ah!
Le voilà.

Ha! ha! ha! ha!
There he is.

MORALÈS
Ah! le voilà! oui, le voilà! etc.
(avec les soldats)
Voyons comment ce tournera.

MORALÈS
Ah, there he is! Yes, there he is! etc.
(With the soldiers)
Let's see how this'll turn out.

The second verse follows and must be faithfully adapted to the scene mimed by the three characters. The young man approaches the old gentleman and the young lady, bows, and exchanges a few words in a low voice, etc.

MORALÈS

MORALÈS

imitating the young man's eager greeting

Vous trouver ici, quel bonheur!	What luck, finding you here!

assuming the old husband's sour-tempered look

Je suis bien votre serviteur!	Your servant!

putting on the young man's manner again

Il salue, il parle avec grâce.	He bows, he turns on the charm.

then the old husband's expression

Le vieux mari fait la grimace;	The old husband pulls a face;

imitating the lady's simpering smiles

Mais d'un air très encourageant La dame accueille le galant.	but the lady is greeting the lover in a very encouraging manner.

At this moment the young man draws from his pocket a note which he shows to the lady. The husband, the wife, and the young blade all three slowly take a little stroll on the square, the young man endeavoring to slip his love-letter to the lady.

MORALÈS
Ils font ensemble quelques pas;
Notre amoureux, levant le bras,
fait voir au mari quelque chose,

MORALÈS
They walk a few steps together;
our lovebird, raising his arm,
draws the husband's attention to somthing,

The young man, with one hand, points out something in the sky to the old gentleman, and with the other passes his note to the lady

Et le mari, toujours morose,
Regarde en l'air . . . Le tour est fait,
car la dame a pris le billet!
Et voilà! Et voilà! Ah! ah!
On voit comment ça tournera!
(avec les soldats)

and the husband, still morose,
looks up in the air . . . The trick has worked,
for the lady has taken the note.
And that's that! that's that! Ha! Ha!
We see how that'll turn out!
(with the soldiers)

On voit comment ça tournera!
Ah! ah! ah! ah!
On voit comment ça tournera! etc.

We see how that'll turn out!
Ha! ha! ha! ha!
We see how that'll turn out! etc.

Scene Two **MARCH AND CHORUS OF STREET BOYS** *A military march of bugles and fifes is heard in the distance. The relief guard is arriving. The old gentleman and the young man exchange a cordial handshake, and the young man bows respectfully to the lady. An officer comes out of the guard-house. Soldiers take their muskets and form up in front of the guard-house. The passers-by gather in a group to watch the parade. The military march comes nearer and nearer. At last the relief guard emerges and crosses the bridge. First, two bugles and two fifes. Then a band of street urchins. Behind the children, Lieutenant Zuniga and Corporal Don José, then the troopers.*

CHOEUR DES GAMINS
Avec la garde montante,
Nous arrivons, nous voilà.
Sonne, trompette éclatante!
Taratata, taratata!
Nous marchons la tête haute
Comme de petits soldats,
Marquant sans faire de faute,
Une, deux, marquant le pas.
Les épaules en arrière
Et la poitrine en dehors,
Les bras de cette maniére
Tombant tout le long du corps.
Avec la garde montante, etc.

CHORUS OF STREET BOYS
Right beside the relief guard,
here we come, here we are!
Blow out, loud trumpet!
Taratata, taratata!
We march with head erect
like little soldiers,
keeping time with no mistakes—
one, two—keeping step.
Shoulders back
and chest well out,
arms this way
straight down beside the body.
Right beside the relief guard, etc.

The relief guard halts facing the guard going off duty. The officers salute with their swords and begin to talk in low voices. The sentries are changed.

MORALÈS *(à Don José)*
Il y a une jolie fille qui est venue to demander. Elle a dit qu'elle reviendrait. . . .

MORALÈS *(to Don José)*
There's a pretty girl been asking for you.
She said she'd come back. . . .

53

JOSÉ
Une jolie fille?

MORALÈS
Oui, et gentiment habillée, une jupe bleue,
des nattes tombant sur les épaules. . . .

JOSÉ
C'est Micaëla. Ce ne peut être que Micaëla.

MORALÈS
Elle n'a pas dit son nom.

REPRISE DU CHOEUR DES GAMINS
Et la garde descendante
Rentre chez elle et s'en va.
Sonne, trompette éclatante,
Taratata, taratata!
Nous marchons la tête haute
Comme de petits soldats, etc.

JOSÉ
A pretty girl?

MORALÈS
Yes, and nicely dressed, a blue skirt, plaits
down over her shoulders. . . .

JOSÉ
It's Micaëla. It can only be Micaëla.

MORALÈS
She didn't give her name.

CHORUS OF STREET BOYS *(reprise)*
And the old guard
goes off home to barracks.
Blow out, loud trumpet!
Taratata, taratata!
We march with head erect
like little soldiers, etc.

*Soldiers, urchins, and idlers go off at the back; the sound of chorus, fifes, and bugles
grows fainter. The commander of the new guard, during this time, inspects his men
silently. When the chorus of street boys can no longer be heard, the soldiers are dis-
missed and enter the guard-house. Don José and Zuniga remain.*

ZUNIGA
Dites-moi, brigadier? Qu'est-ce que c'est
que ce grand bâtiment?

JOSÉ
C'est la manufacture de tabacs . . .

ZUNIGA
Ce sont des femmes qui travaillent là? . . .

ZUNIGA
Tell me, corporal, what's that great
building?

JOSÉ
It's the tobacco factory . . .

ZUNIGA
It's women who work there? . . .

JOSÉ
Oui, mon lieutenant. Elles n'y sont pas
maintenant tout à l'heure, après leur dîner,
elles vont revenir. Il y aura du monde pour
les voir passer.

ZUNIGA
Il y en a de jeunes?

JOSÉ
Mais oui, mon lieutenant.

ZUNIGA
Et de jolies?

JOSÉ *(en riant)*
Je le suppose . . . je n'ai les ai jamais beaucoup regardées . . .

ZUNIGA
Allons donc! . . .

JOSÉ
. . . ces Andalouses me font peur, toujours
à railler . . . jamais un mot de raison. . .

ZUNIGA
Et puis nous avons un faible pour les jupes
bleues et pour les nattes tombant sur les
épaules . . .

JOSÉ *(riant)*
Ah! mon lieutenant a entendu ce que disait
Moralès?

JOSÉ
Yes, sir. They're not there now presently,
after their dinner, they'll come back.
Everyone'll be here to see them go by.

ZUNIGA
There are young ones?

JOSÉ
Why yes, sir.

ZUNIGA
And pretty ones?

JOSÉ *(laughing)*
I suppose so . . . I've never taken much
notice of them . . .

ZUNIGA
Get away with you! . . .

JOSÉ
These Andalusian girls frighten me . . .
always making fun of you . . . never a word
of sense . . .

ZUNIGA
And then we've got a weakness for blue
skirts and for pigtails down over the shoulders . . .

JOSÉ *(laughing)*
Ah, sir, so you heard what Moralès said?

ZUNIGA

Oui . . .

JOSÉ

Je ne le nierai pas . . . la jupe bleu, les nattes, c'est le costume de la Navarre . . . ça me rappelle le pays . . .

ZUNIGA

Vous êtes Navarrais?

JOSÉ

Et vieux chrétien. Malheureusement, j'aimais trop jouer à la paume . . . Un jour, un gars me chercha querelle; j'eus encore l'avantage, mais cela m'obligea de quitter le pays. Je me fis soldat! Ma mère me suivit et vint s'établir à dix lieues de Séville . . . avec la petite Micaëla. . .

ZUNIGA

Et quel âge a-t-elle, la petite Micaëla?

JOSÉ

Dix-sept ans.

ZUNIGA

Il fallait dire cela tout de suite . . . Je comprends maintenant pourquoi vous ne pouvez pas me dire si les ouvrières sont jolies ou laides.

The factory bell is heard.

JOSÉ

Voici la cloche qui sonne, mon lieutenant, vous allez pouvoir juger pour vous-même. .

ZUNIGA

Yes . . .

JOSÉ

I won't deny it . . . blue skirt, pigtails, it's the dress of Navarra . . . that reminds me of home . . .

ZUNIGA

You're from Navarra?

JOSÉ

And from an old Christian family. Unfortunately I was too fond of playing paume* . . . one day a lad picked a quarrel with me; I came off best again, but this forced me to leave the country. I went for a soldier! My mother followed me and came to settle ten leagues from Seville . . . with the little Micaëla.

ZUNIGA

And how old is the little Micaëla?

JOSÉ

Seventeen.

ZUNIGA

You should have said that at once. . . . Now I understand why you can't tell me whether the factory-girls are pretty or ugly.

JOSÉ

There's the bell ringing, sir, you'll be able to judge for yourself. . . . As for me, I'm

* A kind of fives.

. . Quant à moi, je vais faire une chaîne
pour attacher mon épinglette.

going to make a chain for fixing my priming-pin.

Scene Three   **CHORUS OF CIGARETTE GIRLS** *The square fills up with young men who have come to intercept the cigarette girls. The soldiers come out of the guard-house. Don José sits down on a seat, and remains quite indifferent to all the comings and goings, working on a little chain for his priming-pin.*

JEUNES GENS
La cloche a sonné; nous, des ouvrières
nous venons ici guetter le retour;
et nous vous suivrons, brunes cigarières,
en vous murmurant des propos d'amour!

YOUNG MEN
The bell has rung; we've come here to
catch the factory-girls on their way back;
and we'll follow you, dark-haired cigarette
girls, murmuring words of love to you!

At this point the girls appear, smoking cigarettes.

LES SOLDATS
Voyez-les! Regards impudents,
mines coquettes,
fumant toutes du bout des dents la cigarette.

SOLDIERS
Look at them! Impudent glances,
saucy airs,
all of them puffing away at a cigarette.

LES CIGARIÈRES
Dans l'air, nous suivons des yeux
la fumée, la fumée,
qui vers les cieux
monte, monte parfumée.
Cela monte gentiment
à la tête, à la tête,
toute doucement
cela vous met l'âme en fête!
Le doux parler des amants,
c'est fumée!
Leurs transports et leurs serments,
c'est fumée!
Dans l'air, nous suivons des yeux
la fumée, etc.

CIGARETTE GIRLS
We gaze after the smoke
as it rises in the air,
sweet-smelling,
towards the skies.
Gracefully it mounts
to your head,
so gently
it exhilarates you!
Lovers' soft talk—
it's smoke!
Their raptures and promises—
smoke!
We gaze after the smoke
as it rises, etc.

LES SOLDATS	SOLDIERS
Mais nous ne voyons pas la Carmencita!	But we don't see La Carmencita!

Carmen enters

LES CIGARIÈRES ET LES JEUNES GENS	CIGARETTE GIRLS AND YOUNG MEN
La voilà!	There she is!
La voilà!	There she is!
Voilà la Carmencita!	There's La Carmencita!

She has a bunch of acacia flowers at her bodice, and a acacia flower in the corner of her mouth. The young men come in with Carmen. They follow her, surround her, talk to her. She flirts with them in an offhand fashion. Don José looks up. He glances at Carmen and then quietly resumes his work.

LES JEUNES GENS	YOUNG MEN
Carmen! sur tes pas, nous nous pressons tous!	Carmen, we all throng after you!
Carmen! sois gentille, au moins réponds-nous	Carmen, be kind, answer us at least,
et dis-nous quel jour tu nous aimeras!	and tell us when you're going to love us!

disc no. 1/track 5   *Quand je vous aimerai? ... L'amour est un oiseau rebelle*

(*Habanera*) A habanera is not a Spanish but a Cuban musical form. It was inspired and inventive for Bizet to borrow the basic melody, a Hispanic-American dance rhythm, from a song popular in France at that time. In what is perhaps Carmen's most unforgettable aria **(00:31)**, the gently rocking habanera suggests a mysterious allure that reaches back into ancient and elusive cultures, which sound part gypsy and part Moorish to the modern listener.

CARMEN *(regardent Don José)*	CARMEN *(with a glance at Don José)*
Quand je vous aimerai?	When I'm going to love you?
Ma foi, je ne sais pas.	My word, I don't know.
Peut-être jamais, peut-être demain;	Perhaps never, perhaps tomorrow;
mais pas aujourd'hui, c'est certain.	but not today, that's certain.

HABANERA

GRACE BUMBRY IN A 1968–69 PRODUCTION OF CARMEN AT THE METROPOLITAN OPERA.

CARMEN

L'amour est un oiseau rebelle
que nul ne peut apprivoiser,
et c'est bien en vain qu'on l'appelle,
s'il lui convient de refuser.
Rien n'y fait, menace ou prière,
l'un parle bien, l'autre se tait;
et c'est l'autre que je préfère
il n'a rien dit, mais il me plaît.
L'amour! etc.

CHOEUR

L'amour est un oiseau rebelle, etc.

CARMEN

L'amour est enfant de bohème,
il n'a jamais connu de loi
Si tu ne m'aimes pas, je t'aime;
si je t'aime, prends garde à toi! etc.

CARMEN

Love is a rebellious bird
that no one can tame,
and it's quite useless to call him
if it suits him to refuse.
Nothing moves him, neither threat nor
plea, one man speaks freely, the other keeps
mum; and it's the other one I prefer
he's said nothing, but I like him.
Love! etc.

CHORUS

Love is a rebellious bird, etc.

CARMEN

Love is a gypsy child,
he has never heard of law.
If you don't love me, I love you;
if I love you, look out for yourself! etc.

CHOEUR
Prends garde à toi! etc.
L'amour est enfant de bohème, etc.

CARMEN
L'oiseau que to croyais surprendre
battit de l'aile et s'envola—
l'amour est loin, tu peux l'attendre;
tu ne l'attends plus il est là!
Tout autour de toi vite, vite,
il vient, s'en va, puis il revient—
tu crois le tenir, il t'évite,
tu crois l'éviter, il te tient.
L'amour! etc.

CHOEUR
Tout autour de toi, etc.

CARMEN
L'amour est enfant de bohème,
il n'a jamais connu de loi.
Si tu ne m'aimes pas, je t'aime;
si je t'aime, prends garde à toi!
Si tu ne m'aimes pas, je t'aime, etc.

CHOEUR
Prends garde à toi! etc.
L'amour est enfant de bohème, etc.

CHORUS
Look out for yourself! etc.
Love is a gypsy child, etc.

CARMEN
The bird you thought to catch unawares
beat its wings and away it flew—
love's far away, and you can wait for it;
you wait for it no longer—and there it is.
All around you, quickly, quickly,
it comes, it goes, then it returns—
you think you can hold it, it evades you,
you think to evade it, it holds you fast.
Love! etc.

CHORUS
All around you, etc.

CARMEN
Love is a gypsy child,
he has never heard of law.
If you don't love me, I love you;
if I love you, look out for yourself!
If you don't love me, I love you, etc.

CHORUS
Look out for yourself! etc.
Love is a gypsy child, etc.

Scene Five   **SCENE**

disc no. 1/track 6   *Carmen! sur tes pas, nous nous pressons tous!* In the moment following the habanera, Carmen ponders which man might be the recipient of her acacia flower. She looks beyond the men who desire her to one who does not, the otherwise engaged Don José **(00:13)**. As she approaches him, the accompaniment is reduced to a sustained note in the violas **(00:41)**, followed by a dissonant slap of a chord as Carmen tosses the flower at José, laughs, and runs away.

JEUNES GENS
Carmen! sur tes pas, nous nous pressons tous!
Carmen! sois gentille, au moins réponds-nous!

YOUNG MEN
Carmen, we all throng after you!
Carmen, be kind, answer us at least!

> *A pause. The young men surround Carmen, who looks at them one by one. Then she breaks through the circle and goes straight to Don José, who is still busied with his little chain.*

CARMEN
Qu'est-ce tu fais là? . . .

CARMEN
What are you up to there? . . .

JOSÉ
Je fais une chaîne pour attacher mon épinglette.

JOSÉ
I'm making a chain to fix my priming-pin.

CARMEN
Ton épinglette, vraiment! Ton épinglette. . . épinglier de mon âme . . .

CARMEN
Your priming-pin, really! Your priming pin. . . . Pin-maker of my heart . . .

> *Carmen throws the acacia flower at Don José. He jumps up. The flower has fallen at his feet. Outburst of general laughter.*

LES CIGARIERÈS

CIGARETTE GIRLS

> *surrounding Don José*

L'amour est enfant de bohème, etc.

Love is a gypsy child, etc.

> *The factory bell rings again. Carmen and the other cigarette girls run into the factory. Exeunt young men, etc. The soldiers go into the guard-house, followed by the lieutenant, who had been chatting to two or three of the girls. Don José is left alone.*

JOSÉ
Qu'est-ce cela veut dire, ces façons-là? . . .
Quelle effronterie!

JOSÉ
What's all that mean?—all those carryings-on? . . . What shamelessness!

> *He looks at the acacia flower on the ground at his feet. He picks it up.*

Avec quelle adresse elle me l'a lancée, cette fleur. . .

How cleverly she threw it at me, this flower . . .

He smells the flower.

S'il y a des sorcières, cette fille-là en est une.

If there are witches, *that* girl is one.

Enter Micaëla

ENRICO CARUSO AS
DON JOSÉ.

disc no. 1/track 7 *Monsieur mon brigadier? . . . Ma mère, je la vois*

The duet of Don José and Micaëla brings some relief after the raw sexual tension that has been building steadily since the curtain rose on Act I. The music is unabashedly sweet, even bucolic in its sound **(00:19)**, reflecting Don José's sentimental feelings for home, for his mother **(00:35)**, and for the virginal Micaëla who has come to find him. Like the rest of the music in the score associated with Micaëla (a character who does not appear in Merimée's novella), this duet is in a style typical of the French opera then—fluently melodic and tender in its expression **(03:46)**, yet not as overtly passionate as the Italian style.

MICAËLA
Monsieur le brigadier?

JOSÉ

hurriedly concealing the acacia flower

Qu'est-ce que c'est? . . . Micaëla! . . . Tu viens de là-bas? . . .

MICAËLA
C'est votre mère qui m'envoie. . .

Scene Six   **DUET**

JOSÉ
Parle-moi de ma mère!

MICAËLA
J'apporte de sa part, fidèle messagère, cette lettre. . .

JOSÉ
Une lettre! etc.

MICAËLA
Et puis un peu d'argent
pour ajouter à votre traitement.
Et puis . . .

JOSÉ
Et puis?

MICAËLA
Et puis . . . vraiment je n'ose,

MICAËLA
Corporal?

JOSÉ

What's this? . . . Micaëla! . . . You've come from back there? . . .

MICAËLA
It's your mother who sends me . . .

JOSÉ
Tell me about my mother!

MICAËLA
A faithful messenger, I bring from her this letter . . .

JOSÉ
A letter! etc.

MICAËLA
And then a little money to add to your pay.
And then . . .

JOSÉ
And then?

MICAËLA
And then . . . really, I dare not,

et puis encore une autre chose
qui vaut mieux que l'argent
qui pour un bon fils
aura sans doute plus de prix.

JOSÉ
Cette autre chose, quelle est-elle?
Parle donc.

MICAËLA
Oui, je parlerai;
ce que l'on m'a donné
je vous le donnerai.
Votre mère avec moi sortait de la chapelle,
et c'est alors qu'en m'embrassant;
"Tu vas", m'a-t-elle dit, "t'en aller à la ville;
la route n'est pas longue, une fois à Séville,
tu chercheras mon fils, mon José, mon
enfant.
Et tu lui diras que sa mère
songe nuit et jour à l'absent,
qu'elle regrette et qu'elle espère,
qu'elle pardonne et qu'elle attend.
Tout cela, n'est-ce pas, mignonne,
de ma part tu le lui diras;
et ce baiser que je te donne
de ma part tu le lui rendras."

JOSÉ (*très ému*)
Un baiser de ma mère!

MICAËLA
Un baiser pour son fils!
José, je vous le rends,
comme je l'ai promis.

and then yet another thing
worth more than money
and which a good son will surely value
higher.

JOSÉ
This other thing, what is it?
Tell me, then.

MICAËLA
Yes, I'll tell you;
what was given to me
I'll give to you.
Your mother and I were coming out of the
chapel,
And then, as she kissed me,
"You will go to town," she said.
"it's not far; once in Seville
you'll seek out my son, my José, my boy.
And you'll tell him that his mother
thinks night and day of her absent one,
that she grieves and hopes,
that she forgives and waits.
All that, little one,
you'll tell him from me, won't you;
and this kiss that I'm giving you
you'll give him from me."

JOSÉ (*very moved*)
A kiss from my mother!

MICAËLA
A kiss for her son!
José, I give it to you
as I promised.

Micaëla raises herself on tiptoe and gives Don José a frank, motherly kiss. José, very moved, lets her. He gazes into her eyes. There is a moment of silence.

JOSÉ

Ma mère, je la vois!
Oui, je revois mon village!
O souvenirs d'autrefois,
doux souvenirs du pays!
Doux souvenirs du pays!
O souvenirs chéris!
Vous remplissez mon coeur
de force et de courage!
O souvenirs chéris!
Ma mère, je la vois,
je revois mon village!

MICAËLA

Sa mère, il la revoit!
Il revoit sa village!
O souvenirs d'autrefois!
Souvenirs du pays!
Vous remplissez son coeur
de force et de courage!
O souvenirs chéris!
Sa mère, il la revoit,
il revoit son village!

JOSÉ

his eyes fixed on the factory

Qui sait de quel démon
j'allais être la proie!
Même de loin, ma mère me défend,
et ce baiser qu'elle m'envoie
écarte le péril et suave son enfant!

JOSÉ

I see my mother!
Yes, I see my village again!
O memories of bygone days,
sweet memories of home!
Sweet memories of home!
O precious memories!
You put back strength
and courage into my heart!
O precious memories!
I see my mother,
I see my village again!

MICAËLA

He sees his mother again!
He sees his village again!
O memories of bygone days!
Memories of home!
You put back strength
and courage into his heart!
O precious memories!
He sees his mother again,
he sees his village again!

JOSÉ

Who knows into what demon's clutches
I was about to fall!
Even from afar my mother protects me
and this kiss she sent me
wards off the peril and saves her son!

MICAËLA
Quel démon? quel péril?
Je ne comprends pas bien.
Que veut dire cela?

JOSÉ
Rien! Rien!
Parlons de toi, la messagère.
Tu vas retourner au pays?

MICAËLA
Oui, ce soir même
demain je verrai votre mère.

JOSÉ
Tu la verras!
Et bien, tu lui diras
que son fils l'aime et la vénère
et qu'il se repent aujourd'hui;
il veut que là-bas sa mère
soit contente de lui!
Tout cela, n'est-ce pas, mignonne,
de ma part, tu le lui diras,
et ce baiser que je te donne,
de ma part tu le lui rendras.

He kisses her.

MICAËLA
Oui, je vous le promets, de la part de son fils
José je le rendrai comme je l'ai promis.

JOSÉ
Ma mère, je la vois! etc.

MICAËLA
Sa mère, il la revoit! etc.

MICAËLA
What demon? What peril?
I don't quite understand.
What do you mean by that?

JOSÉ
Nothing! Nothing!
Let's talk about you, the messenger.
You're going back home?

MICAËLA
Yes, this very evening
tomorrow I shall see your mother.

JOSÉ
You'll be seeing her!
Well then, you'll tell her—
that her son loves and reveres her
and that today he is repentant;
he wants his mother back there
to be pleased with him!
All this, my sweet,
you'll tell her from me, won't you, and this
kiss that I give you
you'll give her from me.

MICAËLA
Yes, I promise you; from her son
José I shall give it as I have promised.

JOSÉ
I see my mother! etc.

MICAËLA
He sees his mother again! etc.

Attends un peu maintenant In the original production, the chorus that describes the fight in the cigarette factory **(00:25)** left the ladies of the Opéra-Comique's original ensemble in a state of frenzy. Already tested by the smoking chorus that introduced them earlier, they were not only required to sing this particularly intricate ensemble, they had to be physically boisterous as well. (Their preferred manner of performing was to stand facing forward and simply sing.) It is a stunning moment, as bloodthirsty and gritty as anything in Italian verismo opera, with Bizet neatly catching the visceral, almost carnal excitement **(02:30)** the fight has aroused in its witnesses.

JOSÉ

Attends un peu maintenant. . . je vais lire sa lettre . . .

MICAËLA

Je viens de me rappeler que votre mère m'a chargée de quelques petits achats . . .

JOSÉ

Attends un peu . . .

MICAËLA

Non, non . . . je reviendrai, j'aime mieux cela . . . je reviendrai, je reviendrai . . .

She goes out.

JOSÉ

reading

"Il n'y en a pas qui t'aime davantage . . . et si tu voulais. . . ." Oui, ma mère, oui, j'épouserai Micaëla. Quant à cette bohèmienne, avec ses fleurs qui ensorcellent . . .

JOSÉ

Wait a bit now. . . I'm going to read her letter . . .

MICAËLA

I've just remembered that your mother asked me to make a few small purchases for her . . .

JOSÉ

Wait a little while . . .

MICAËLA

No, no . . . I'll come back, I'd rather do that . . . I'll come back, I'll come back . . .

JOSÉ

"There's not one of them who loves you more . . . and if you wanted to. . . ." Yes, mother, yes, I'll marry Micaëla. As for that gypsy with her flowers that bewitch . . .

Just as he is about to tear the flower from his tunic, an uproar begins in the factory.
Zuniga comes on stage, followed by soldiers.

ZUNIGA
Eh bien! eh bien! qu'est-ce qui arrive? . . .

ZUNIGA
Well now, well, what's happening? . . .

Scene Seven　　　**CHORUS**

PREMIER GROUPE DE FEMMES
Au secours! Au secours!
N'entendez-vous pas?

FIRST GROUP OF GIRLS
Help! Help!
Can't you hear?

DEUXIÈME GROUPE DE FEMMES
Au secours! Au secours!
Messieurs les soldats!

SECOND GROUP OF GIRLS
Help! Help!
You soldiers!

PREMIER GROUPE DE FEMMES
C'est la Carmencita!

FIRST GROUP OF GIRLS
It's Carmencita!

DEUXIÈME GROUPE DE FEMMES
Non, non, ce n'est pas elle!
Pas du tout!

SECOND GROUP OF GIRLS
No, no, it's not her!
Not a bit of it!

PREMIER GROUPE DE FEMMES
C'est elle! Si fait, si fait, c'est elle!
Elle a porté les premiers coups!

FIRST GROUP OF GIRLS
It's her! It is, it is! It's her!
She started the fighting!

DEUXIÈME GROUPE DE FEMMES
Ne les écoutez pas!

SECOND GROUP OF GIRLS
Don't listen to them!

TOUTES LES FEMMES

ALL THE GIRLS

surrounding Zuniga

Ecoutez-nous, monsieur!
Ecoutez-nous! etc.

DEUXIÈME GROUPE DE FEMMES

pulling the officer to their side

La Manuelita disait,
et répétait à voix haute
qu'elle achèterait sans faute
un âne que lui plaisait.

PREMIER GROUPE DE FEMMES
Alors la Carmencita,
railleuse à son ordinaire,
dit "Un âne, pourquoi faire?
Un balai te suffira."

DEUXIÈME GROUPE DE FEMMES
Manuelita riposta
et dit à sa camarade
"Pour certaine promenade,
mon âne te servira!—"

PREMIER GROUPE DE FEMMES
"—Et ce jour-là tu pourras
à bon droit faire la fière;
deux laquais suivront derrière,
t'émouchant à tour de bras!"

TOUTES LES FEMMES
Là-dessus, toutes les deux
se sont prises aux cheveux!

ZUNIGA
Au diable tout ce bavardage!

SECOND GROUP OF GIRLS

Manuelita said, and kept saying
at the top of her voice,
that she'd make sure she bought
a donkey that pleased her.

FIRST GROUP OF GIRLS
Then Carmencita,
in her usual mocking way,
said "A donkey? What for?
A broom will do for you."

SECOND GROUP OF GIRLS
Manuelita retorted,
and said to her friend
"For a certain ride
my donkey will be useful to you!—"

FIRST GROUP OF GIRLS
"—And on that day you'll be able
to play the lady in your own right;
two lackeys will follow behind
keeping flies off as best they can!"

ALL THE GIRLS
Thereupon they both started
to pull each other's hair out!

ZUNIGA
To the devil with all this chatter!

Prenez, José, deux hommes avec vous
et voyez là-dedans qui cause ce tapage.

José, take two men in with you
and see who's causing all this commotion.

*Don José takes two men with him. The soldiers go into the factory. All this while the
girls are pushing and arguing among themselves.*

PREMIER GROUPE DE FEMMES
C'est la Carmencita! etc.

FIRST GROUP OF GIRLS
It's Carmencita! etc.

DEUXIÈME GROUPE DE FEMMES
Non, non, ce n'est pas elle! etc.

SECOND GROUP OF GIRLS
No, no! It's not her! etc.

ZUNIGA
Holà!
Eloignez-moi toutes ces femmes-là!

ZUNIGA
Stop!
Rid me of all these women!

TOUTES LES FEMMES
Monsieur! Ne les écoutez pas! etc.

ALL THE GIRLS
Sir, don't listen to them! etc.

*The soldiers keep the girls back. Carmen appears at the factory door, led by Don
José and followed by two dragoons.*

The factory-girls go out in a disorderly rush.

ZUNIGA
Voyons, brigadier . . . Maintenant que nous
avons un peu de silence . . . qu'est-ce que
vous avez trouvé là-dedans?

ZUNIGA
Let's see, corporal . . . now that we've got a
moment's silence . . . what did you find
inside there?

JOSÉ
J'ai trouvé trois cents femmes, hurlant, ges-
ticulant. Il y en avait une qui avait sur la
figure un X qu'on venait de lui marquer en
deux coups de couteau . . . en face de la
blessée . . .

JOSÉ
I found three hundred women, yelling and
waving their arms about. There was one
who had an X on her face that someone
had just carved on her with two knife-
slashes. . . . Facing the wounded girl . . .

On a glance from Carmen he stops.

ZUNIGA
Eh bien?

JOSÉ
J'ai vu mademoiselle . . .

ZUNIGA
Mademoiselle Carmencita?

JOSÉ
Oui, mon lieutenant.

ZUNIGA
Et qu'est-ce qu'elle disait, mademoiselle
Carmencita?

JOSÉ
Elle ne disait rien, elle serrait les dents et
roulait des yeux comme un caméleon.

ZUNIGA
Well?

JOSÉ
I saw the señorita . . .

ZUNIGA
The señorita Carmencita?

JOSÉ
Yes, sir.

ZUNIGA
And what was she saying, the señorita
Carmencita?

JOSÉ
She wasn't saying anything, she was gritting
her teeth and rolling her eyes like a
chameleon.

*The lieutenant looks at Carmen; she, after a glance at Don José and a slight shrug
of her shoulders, has become impassive again.*

JOSÉ
J'ai prié mademoiselle de me suivre. . . .

JOSÉ
I asked the señorita to come with me . . .

Carmen turns sharply and looks at José once more.

SONG AND MELODRAMA

disc no. 1/track 9   *Eh bien!... vous avez entendu?... Tra la la la*   Zuniga demands answers from Carmen, whose contemptuous defiance is dazzling. She sings nonsense in his face **(00:09)**, daring him to cut her, burn her, whatever he wishes, but she will tell him nothing. There follows a section called a melodrama, in which Bizet underscored (as in a film score) **(01:38)** a section leading to spoken dialogue between Carmen and Don José, who is now charged with guarding her. The melodrama is often cut, though it appears in this recording to expand on what is a key moment in the relationship of Carmen and Don José.

ZUNIGA *(à Carmen)*
Eh bien! . . . vous avez entendu? . . . Avez-vous quelque chose à répondre? . . . parlez, j'attends . . .

ZUNIGA *(to Carmen)*
Well! . . . you heard? . . . Have you anything to answer? . . . Speak, I'm waiting . . .

Instead of replying, Carmen starts to sing.

CARMEN
Tra la la la, etc.
Coupe-moi, brûle-moi, je ne te dirai rien.
Tra la la la, etc.
Je brave tout, le feu, le fer et le ciel même.

CARMEN
Tra la la la, etc.
Cut me, burn me, I shall tell you nothing.
Tra la la la, etc.
I defy everything—fire, the sword and heaven itself.

ZUNIGA
Ce ne sont pas des chansons que je te demande, c'est une réponse.

ZUNIGA
It's not songs I'm asking you for, it's a reply.

CARMEN
Tra la la la, etc.
Mon secret je le garde et je le garde bien!
Tra la la la, etc.
J'en aime un autre et meurs en disant que je l'aime.

CARMEN
Tra la la la, etc.
I'm keeping my secret and keeping it close!
Tra la la la, etc.
I love another and I die in saying that I love him.

ZUNIGA

Ah! ah! nous le prenons sur ce ton-là . . . *à José* Ce qui est sûr, n'est-ce pas, c'est qu'il y eu des coups de couteau, et que c'est elle qui les a donnés . . .

ZUNIGA

Aha! So that's the attitude we're taking . . . *to José* What's certain, isn't it, is that there had been a knife attack and that it's she who made it . . .

At this moment five or six women on the right succeed in breaking the line of sentries and rush on to the stage shouting, "Yes, yes, it's her!" One of these women finds herself close by Carmen, who raises her hand and attempts to throw herself upon the woman. Don José stops Carmen. The soldiers haul the women off and this time force them back completely off the stage. A few sentinels remain in sight, guarding the approaches to the square.

ZUNIGA

Eh! vous avez la main leste décidément. (*Aux soldats*) Trouvez-moi une corde.

ZUNIGA

Eh! decidedly you have a ready hand. (*to the soldiers*) Find me a cord.

There is a moment of silence during which Carmen begins humming again in the most impertinent fashion as she watches the officer.

JOSE

Voilà, mon lieutenant.

JOSE

Here it is, sir.

ZUNIGA

Prenez et attachez-moi ces deux jolies mains.

ZUNIGA

Take this and tie those two pretty hands together for me.

Without offering the least resistance, Carmen smilingly holds out her two hands to Don José.

C'est dommage vraiment, car elle est gentille . . . si gentille que vous soyez, vous n'en irez pas moins faire un tour à la prison. Vous pourrez y chanter vos chansons de Bohémienne. Le porte-clefs vous dira ce qu'il en pense.

It's a shame, really, for she's pretty . . . But pretty as you may be, you're nonetheless going to take a stroll to the prison. You can sing your gypsy songs there. The turnkey'll tell you what he thinks of them.

Carmen's hands are bound and she is made to sit down on a stool in front of the guard-house. She remains motionless, her eyes cast down.

Je vais écrire l'ordre. *(à Don José)* C'est vous qui la conduirez . . .

I'm going to write out the order. *(to Don José)* It's you who will take her . . .

He goes out.

CARMEN
Où me conduirez-vous?

CARMEN
Where are you taking me?

JOSÉ
A la prison, ma pauvre enfant . . .

JOSÉ
To the jail, my poor child . . .

CARMEN
Hélas! que deviendrai-je? Seigneur officier, ayez pitié de moi . . . vous êtes si gentil. Laisse-moi m'échapper, je te donnerai un morceau de la *bar lachi*, une petite pierre qui te fera aimer de toutes les femmes.

CARMEN
Alas, what will become of me? Noble officer, take pity on me . . . You are so nice. Let me escape and I'll give you a piece of the *bar lachi*, a little stone which will make you loved by all women.

JOSÉ

JOSÉ

moving away

Nous ne sommes pas ici pour dire des balivernes . . . Il faut aller à la prison. C'est la consigne, et il n'y a pas de remède.

We're not here to talk twaddle . . . We must go to the jail. Those are my instructions, and there's no help for it.

CARMEN
Camarade, mon ami, ne ferez-vous rien pour une payse?

CARMEN
Comrade of my heart, won't you do anything for a fellow-countrywoman?

JOSÉ
Vous êtes Navarraise, vous?

JOSÉ
You're from Navarra, *you?*

CARMEN
Sans doute.

JOSÉ
Allons donc . . . il n'y a pas un mot de vrai
. . . vos yeux seuls, votre bouche, votre teint
. . . tout vous dit Bohémienne . . .

CARMEN
Bohémienne, tu crois?

JOSÉ
J'en suis sûr.

CARMEN
Au fait, je suis bien bonne de me donner la
peine de mentir . . . Oui, je suis
Bohémienne, mais tu n'en feras pas moins
ce que je te demande . . . tu le feras parce
que tu m'aimes . . .

JOSÉ
Moi!

CARMEN
Eh! Oui, tu m'aimes. Cette fleur que tu as
gardée—oh! Tu peux la jeter maintenant . . .
cela n'y fera rien. La charme a opéré . . .

JOSÉ *(avec colère)*
Ne me parle plus, tu entends, je te défends
de me parler.

CARMEN
Certainly.

JOSÉ
Come off it! . . . There's not a word of
truth in it . . . your eyes alone, your
mouth, your colouring . . . everything pro-
claims you a gypsy . . .

CARMEN
A gypsy, you think?

JOSÉ
I'm sure of it.

CARMEN
In fact, I am very simple to go to the trouble of lying . . . Yes, I'm a gypsy, but you'll
do what I want nonetheless . . . You'll do it
because you love me . . .

JOSÉ
I!

CARMEN
Ah yes, you love me. That flower you
kept—oh, you can throw it away now . . .
that makes no difference. The charm has
worked . . .

JOSÉ *(angrily)*
Don't talk to me any more, d'you hear, I
forbid you to talk to me.

disc no. 1/track 11 *C'est très bien... Près des remparts de Séville* (Seguedille) Carmen has Don José in her sights, and, though her hands are bound, she sings this alluring aria to seduce him into letting her escape. The aria begins as a seduction, insinuating and a little mysterious, but when Don José agrees to release her, Carmen repeats the melody with a bold, almost manic intensity **(04:09)**, ending the aria with a shout of joy.

CARMEN
C'est très bien, seigneur officier, c'est très bien. Vous me défendez de parler, je ne parlerai plus . . .

CARMEN
That's all right, officer sir, that's all right. You forbid me to talk, I'll not talk any more . . .

She looks at Don José who backs away.

Scene Nine

SEGUIDILLA AND DUET

MARILYN HORNE AS CARMEN AND JAMES MCCRACKEN AS DON JOSÉ IN ACT I.

CARMEN

Près des remparts de Séville,
chez mon ami Lillas Pastia, j'irai danser la séguedille,
et boire du manzanilla.
J'irai chez mon ami Lillas Pastia!
Oui, mais toute seule on s'ennuie,
et les vrais plaisirs sont à deux.
Donc, pour me tenir compagnie,
j'emmènerai mon amoureux!
Mon amoureux . . . il est au diable
je l'ai mis à la porte hier.
Mon pauvre coeur très consolable,
mon coeur est libre comme l'air.
J'ai des galants à la douzaine,
mais ils ne sont pas à mon gré.
Voici la fin de la semaine,
qui veut m'aimer? Je l'aimerai
Qui veut mon âme? Elle est à prendre!
Vous arrivez au bon moment!
Je n'ai guère le temps d'attendre,
car avec mon nouvel amant . . .
Près des remparts de Séville, etc.

JOSÉ

Tais-toi! Je t'avais dit de ne pas me parler!

CARMEN

Je ne te parle pas,
je chante pour moi-même;
et je pense . . . il n'est pas défendu de penser!
Je pense à certain officier,
qui m'aime, et qu'à mon tour,
oui, à mon tour je pourrais bien aimer!

CARMEN

By the ramparts of Seville,
at my friend Lillas Pastia's place,
I'm going to dance the seguidilla
and drink manzanilla.
I'm going to my friend Lillas Pastia's!
Yes, but all alone one gets bored,
and real pleasures are for two.
So, to keep me company,
I shall take my lover!
My lover . . . he's gone to the devil
I showed him the door yesterday.
My poor heart, so consolable—
my heart is as free as air.
I have suitors by the dozen,
but they are not to my liking.
Here we are at week end;
Who wants to love me! I'll love him.
Who wants my heart? It's for the taking!
You've come at the right moment!
I have hardly time to wait,
for with my new lover . . .
By the ramparts of Seville, etc.

JOSÉ

Stop! I told you not to talk to me!

CARMEN

I'm not talking to you,
I'm singing to myself;
and I'm thinking . . . it's not forbidden to think!
I'm thinking about a certain officer
who loves me,
and whom in my turn I might really love!

JOSÉ
Carmen!

CARMEN
Mon officier n'est pas un capitaine,
pas même un lieutenant,
il n'est que brigadier;
mais c'est assez our une bohémienne,
et je daigne m'en contenter!

JOSÉ

untying Carmen's hands

Carmen, je suis comme un homme ivre,
se je cède, si je me livre,
ta promesse, tu la tiendras,
ah! si je t'aime, Carmen, tu m'aimeras?

CARMEN
Oui . . .
Nous danserons la séguedille
en buvant du manzanilla.

JOSÉ
Chez Lillas Pastia . . .
Tu le promets!
Carmen . . .
Tu le promets!

CARMEN
Ah! Près des remparts de Séville, etc.

JOSÉ
Carmen!

CARMEN
My officer's not a captain,
not even a lieutenant,
he's only a corporal;
but that's enough for a gypsy girl
and I'll deign to content myself with him!

JOSÉ

Carmen, I'm like a drunken man,
if I yield, if I give in,
you'll keep your promise?
Ah! If I love you, Carmen, you'll love me?

CARMEN
Yes . . .
We'll dance the seguidilla
while we drink manzanilla.

JOSÉ
at Lillas Pastia's . . .
You promise!
Carmen . . .
You promise!

CARMEN
Ah! By the ramparts of Seville, etc.

Her hands behind her, Carmen goes and re-seats herself on her stool.

Zuniga returns.

FINALE

ZUNIGA *(à José)*
Voici l'ordre; partez.
Et faites bonne garde.

ZUNIGA *(to José)*
Here's the order; off you go now.
And keep a good lookout.

CARMEN *(bas à José)*
En chemin je te pousserai,
je te pousserai aussi fort que je le pourrais . . .
Laisse-toi renverser . . .
le reste me regarde.

CARMEN *(aside to José)*
On the way I shall push you,
I shall push you as hard as I can . . .
Let yourself fall over . . .
The rest is up to me.

Carmen places herself between the two dragoons, with José at her side. The girls and others return onstage, kept back by the soldiers. Carmen crosses the stage, moving towards the bridge.

CARMEN
L'amour est enfant de bohéme,
il n'a jamais connu de loi.
Si tu ne m'aimes pas, je t'aime;
si je t'aime, prends garde à toi!

CARMEN
Love is a gypsy child,
he has never heard of law.
If you don't love me, I love you;
if I love you, look out for yourself!

Arriving at the foot of the bridge, Carmen pushes José, who falls. In the confusion Carmen takes to her heels. At the middle of the bridge she stops for a moment, sends her cord flying over the parapet of the bridge, and escapes, while the cigarette girls, with great shouts of laughter, surround Zuniga.

Act Two

Scene Eleven

GYPSY SONG ∾ *The tavern of Lillas Pastia. Carmen, Mercédès, Frasquita, Lieutenant Zuniga, Moralès, and another lieutenant are there. A meal has just been finished and the table is in disorder. The officers and gypsy girls are smoking. Two gypsies are strumming guitars in a corner of the room; in the middle, two gypsy girls are singing. Carmen, seated, is watching them dance. An officer is talking to her quietly, but she pays him no attention whatsoever. Suddenly she gets up and begins to sing.*

disc no. 1/track 14 *Les tringles des sistres tintaient* *(Chanson bohèmien)* The hypnotic swirl of the Gypsy Song precedes the second act in the orchestral entr'acte, and it is repeated when the curtain rises. Carmen and her friends Frasquita and Mercédès sing and dance to the tune with a growing frenzy for the crowd at Lillas Pastia's. Carmen is at last seen and heard in her element, and the effect is mesmerizing—the beat of the last verse of the Gypsy Song **(02:50)** gets faster and faster until it drops from delirious exhaustion.

CARMEN
Les tringles des sitres tintaient
avec un éclat métallique,
et sur cette étrange musique
les zingarellas se levaient.
Tambours de basque allaient leur train,
et les guitares forcenées
grinçaient sous des mains obsinées,
même chanson, même refrain.
Tralalalala . . .

CARMEN
The sistrums'* rods were jingling
with a metallic clatter,
and at this strange music
the *zingarellas** leapt to their feet.
Tambourines were keeping time
and the frenzied guitars
ground away under persistent hands,
the same song, the same refrain.
Tralalalala . . .

* Sistrum: jingling instrument; rattle used by ancient nations.

* Zingarella: Zingara, Zingaro gypsy (It.).

Les anneaux de cuivre et d'argent
reluisaient sur les peaux bistrées;
d'orange et de rouge zébrées
les étouffes flottaient au vent.
La danse au chant se mariait,
d'abord indécise et timide,
plus vive ensuite et plus rapide,
cela montait, montait, montait!
Tralalalala . . .

Les bohémiens à tour de bras
de leurs instruments faisaient rage,
et cet éblouissant tapage,
ensorcelait les zingaras!
Sous le rythme de la chanson,
ardentes, folles, enfiévrées,
elles se laissaient, enivrées,
emporter par le tourbillon!
Tralalalala . . .

Copper and silver rings
glittered on dusky skins;
orange- and red-striped
dresses floated in the wind.
Dance and song became one—
at first timid and hesitant,
then livelier and faster
it grew and grew and grew!
Tralalalala . . .

The gypsy boys stormed away
on their instruments with all their might,
and this deafening uproar
bewitched the *zingaras!*
Beneath the rhythm of the song,
passionate, wild, fired with excitement,
they let themselves be carried a way, intoxi-
cated, by the whirlwind!
Tralalalala . . .

At the conclusion of the dance Carmen sinks breathless on to a bench. Lillas Pastia begins to circulate among the officers he looks worried.

ZUNIGA
Vous avez quelque chose à nous dire,
maître Lillas Pastia?

PASTIA
Mon Dieu, messieurs . . .

MORALÈS
Parle, voyons . . .

ZUNIGA
You've something to tell us, Master Lillas
Pastia?

PASTIA
My God, gentlemen . . .

MORALÈS
Speak, come now . . .

PASTIA

Il commence à se faire tard . . . et je suis, plus que personne, obligé d'observer les règlements.

MORALÈS

Cela veut dire que to nous mets à la porte! . . .

PASTIA

Oh! Non, messieurs les officiers, oh! non non . . . je vous fais seulement observer que mon auberge devrait être fermée depuis dix minutes . . .

ZUNIGA

Dieu sait ce qu'il s'y passe dans ton auberge, une fois qu'elle est fermée . . .

PASTIA

Oh! Mon lieutenant . . .

ZUNIGA

Enfin, nous avons encore, avant l'appel, le temps d'aller passer une heure au théâtre . . . vous y viendrez avec nous, n'est-ce pas, les belles?

Pastia signs to the gypsy girls to refuse.

FRASQUITA

Non, messieurs les officiers, non, nous restons ici, nous.

ZUNIGA

Comment, vous ne viendrez pas . . .

PASTIA

It's beginning to get late and I, more than anyone, am obliged to observe the regulations.

MORALÈS

That means that you're showing us the door!

PASTIA

Oh no. Officers, oh no! . . . I only remind you that my inn should have been closed ten minutes ago . . .

ZUNIGA

God knows what goes on in your inn after closing time . . .

PASTIA

Oh, sir! . . .

ZUNIGA

Anyway, we still have time before roll-call to pass an hour at the theatre . . . You'll come there with us, eh, girls?

Pastia signs to the gypsy girls to refuse.

FRASQUITA

No, officers, no, we're staying here, we are.

ZUNIGA

What, you're not coming?—

MERCÉDÈS
C'est impossible.

MORALÈS
Mercédès!

MERCÉDÈS
Je regrette . . .

MORALÈS
Frasquita!

FRASQUITA
Je suis désolée . . .

ZUNIGA
Mais toi, Carment, je suis bien sûr que tu
ne refuseras pas . . .

CARMEN
C'est ce qui vous trompe, mon
lieutenant . . . je refuse.

*While the lieutenant is speaking to Carmen, two other lieutenants try to persuade
Frasquita and Mercédès.*

ZUNIGA
Tu m'en veux?

CARMEN
Pourquoi vous en voudrais-je?

ZUNIGA
Parce qu'il y a un mois, j'ai eu la cruauté de
t'envoyer à la prison . . .

MERCÉDÈS
It's impossible.

MORALÈS
Mercédès!

MERCÉDÈS
Sorry . . .

MORALÈS
Frasquita!

FRASQUITA
Ever so sorry . . .

ZUNIGA
But you, Carmen, I'm quite sure you won't
refuse . . .

CARMEN
That's where you're wrong, Lieutenant, I
do refuse.

ZUNIGA
You've got a grudge against me?

CARMEN
Why should I have?

ZUNIGA
Because, a month ago, I was cruel enough
to send you to prison . . .

as though she did not remember

A la prison . . . je ne me souviens pas d'être allée àla prison . . .

To prison? . . . I don't recall having gone to prison.

Zuniga
Je sais pardieu bien que tu n'y es pas allée . . . le brigadier qui était chargé de te conduire ayant jugé à propos de te laisser échapper . . . et de se faire dégrader et imprisonner pour cela . . .

Zuniga
I know jolly well that you didn't go there . . . the corporal who had the job of taking you having opportunely decided to let you escape . . . and to get himself demoted and imprisoned for that . . .

Carmen

Carmen

serious

Dégrader et emprisonner?

Demoted and imprisoned?

Zuniga
Il a passé un mois en prison . . .

Zuniga
He's spent a month in prison . . .

Carmen
Mais il en est sorti?

Carmen
But he's out now?

Zuniga
Depuis hier seulement!

Zuniga
Only since yesterday!

Carmen
Tout est bien, puisqu'il en est sorti, tout est bien.

Carmen
Everything's all right then, since he is out, everything's all right.

Zuniga
A la bonne heure, tu te consoles vite . . .

Zuniga
Well well, you console yourself quickly . . .

CARMEN

Si vous m'en croyez, vous ferez comme moi, vous voulez nous emmener, nous ne voulons pas vous suivre . . . vous vous consolerez . . .

MORALÈS

Il faudra bien.

The scene is interrupted by a chorus sung in the wings.

Scene Twelve **CHORUS AND ENSEMBLE**

CHŒUR

Vivat! vivat le toréro!
Vivat! vivat Escamillo! etc.

The dialogue continues during the singing of the above Chorus.

ZUNIGA

Qu'est-ce que c'est que ça?

MERCÉDÈS

Une promenade aux flambeaux . . .

FRASQUITA

C'est Escamillo . . . un torero qui s'est fait remarquer aux dernières courses de Grenade.

MORALÈS

Pardieu, il faut le faire venir . . . nous boirons en son honneur!

ZUNIGA

C'est cela, je vais l'inviter.

CARMEN

If you take my advice you'll do like me; you want to take us out, we don't want to come with you . . . you will console yourselves . . .

MORALÈS

We'll have to.

CHORUS

Hurrah! Hurrah for the torero!
Hurrah! Hurrah for Escamillo! etc.

ZUNIGA

What's all that?

MERCÉDÈS

A torchlight procession . . .

FRASQUITA

It's Escamillo . . . a bullfighter who distinguished himself at the last Granada meetings.

MORALÈS

By jove, we must get him up here . . . we'll drink in his honour!

ZUNIGA

That's it, I'll invite him.

Monsieur le toréro . . . voulez-vous faire l'amitié de monter ici? Vous y trouverez des gens qui aiment fort tous ceux qui, comme vous ont de l'adresse et du courage.

Señor torero, will you do us the kindness to step up here? You'll find chaps who are very fond of all those, like yourself, who have skill and courage . . .

CHOEUR
Vivat! vivat le toréro!
Vivat! vivat Escamillo! etc.

CHORUS
Hurrah! Hurrah for the torero!
Hurrah! Hurrah for Escamillo! etc.

Enter Escamillo.

ZUNIGA
Nous vous remercions d'avoir accepté notre invitation; nous n'avons pas voulu vous laisser passer sans boire avec vous au grand art de la tauromachie.

ZUNIGA
We thank you for having accepted our invitation; we didn't want to let you go by without drinking with you to the great art of tauromachy.

ESCAMILLO
Messieurs les officiers, je vous remercie.

ESCAMILLO
Gentlemen, I thank you.

Scene Thirteen   **TOREADOR'S SONG**

disc no. 1/track 17   *Votre toast, je peux vous le rendre* (Toreador Song) One of the most famous arias in all of opera, Escamillo's Toreador Song is a celebration of the swaggering macho tradition. The arresting verses are in a minor key. In them, the toreador describes his exploits and their dangers. However, the refrain ("Toréador, en garde . . . ") is in the major. This proud, striding melody **(01:19)** becomes Escamillo's identity as he sings of the love that awaits him when his trials are over.

ESCAMILLO
Votre toast, je peux vous le rendre,

ESCAMILLO
I can return your toast,

señors, car avec les soldats,
oui, les toréros peuvent s'entendre,
pour plaisirs ils ont les combats!
Le cirque est plein, c'est jour de fête,
le cirque est plein du haut en bas.
Les spectateurs perdant la tête,
les spectateurs s'interpellent à grand fracas!
Apostrophes, cris et tapage
poussés jusques à la fureur!
Car c'est la fête du courage!
C'est la fête des gens de coeur!
Allons! en garde! ah!
Toréador, en garde!
Et songe bien, oui, songe en combattant,
qu'un oeil noir te regarde
et que l'amour t'attend!
Toréador, l'amour t'attend!

TOUT LE MONDE
Toréador, en garde! etc.

gentlemen, for soldiers—
yes—and bullfighters understand each
other; fighting is their game!
The ring is packed, it's a holiday,
the ring is full from top to bottom.
The spectators, losing their wits,
yell at each other at the tops of their voices!
Exclamations, cries and uproar
carried to the pitch of fury!
For this is the fiesta of courage,
this is the fiesta of the stouthearted!
Let's go! On guard! Ah!
Toreador, on guard!
And remember, yes, remember as you fight
that two dark eyes are watching you,
that love awaits you!
Toreador, love awaits you!

CHORUS
Toreador, on guard! etc.

Carmen refills Escamillo's glass.

ESCAMILLO
Tout d'un coup, on fait silence,
on fait silence, ah! que se passe-t-il?
Plus de cris, c'est l'instant!
Le taureau s'élance
en bondissant hors du toril!
Il s'élance! Il entre, il frappe!
Un cheval roule, entraînant un picador!
"Ah! bravo Toro!" hurle la foule;
le taureau va, il vient,
il vient et frappe encore!
En secouant ses banderilles,
plein de fureur, il court!
Le cirque est plein de sang!

ESCAMILLO
Suddenly everyone falls silent;
ah—what's happening?
No more shouts, this is the moment!
The bull comes bounding
out of the *toril!*
He charges, comes in, strikes!
A horse rolls over, dragging down a pica-
dor! "Ah! Bravo bull!" roars the crowd;
the bull turns, comes back.
Comes back and strikes again!
Shaking his banderillas,
maddened with rage, he runs about!
The ring is covered with blood!

On se sauve, on franchit les grilles.
C'est ton tour maintenant!
Allons! en garde! ah!
Toréador, en garde! etc.

TOUT LE MONDE
Toréador, en garde! etc.
. . . . l'amour t'attend!

Men jump clear, leap the barriers.
It's your turn now!
Let's go! On guard! Ah!
Toreador, on guard! etc.

CHORUS
Toreador, on guard! etc.
. . . love awaits you!

Scene Thirteen B   CHORUS

FRASQUITA
L'Amour!

FRASQUITA
Love!

ESCAMILLO
L'Amour!

ESCAMILLO
Love!

MERCÉDÈS
L'Amour!

MERCÉDÈS
Love!

ESCAMILLO
L'Amour!

ESCAMILLO
Love!

CARMEN
L'Amour!

CARMEN
Love!

ALL
Toréador! Toréador! L'amour t'attend!

ALL
Toreador, Toreador, love awaits you!

They drink and exchange handshakes with the toreador.

PASTIA
Messieurs les officiers, je vous en prie.

PASTIA
Officers, sirs, I beg you.

ZUNIGA
C'est bien, c'est bien, nous partons.

ZUNIGA
All right, all right, we're going.

ESCAMILLO

Dis-moi ton nom, et la première fois que je frapperai le taureau, ce sera ton nom que je prononcerai.

CARMEN

Je m'appelle la Carmencita.

ESCAMILLO

La Carmencita?

CARMEN

Carmen, la Carmencita, comme tu voudras.

ESCAMILLO

Eh bien! Carmen ou la Carmencita, si je m'avisais de t'aimer et d'être aimé de toi, qu'est-ce tu me répondrais?

CARMEN

Je répondrais que tu peux m'aimer tout à ton aise mais que quant à être aimé de moi pour le moment, il n'y faut pas songer!

ESCAMILLO

J'attendrai alors et me contenterai d'espérer . . .

CARMEN

Il n'est pas défendu d'attendre et il est toujours agréable d'espérer.

ZUNIGA

ESCAMILLO

Tell me your name, and the first time I kill a bull it will be your name that I utter.

CARMEN

I'm called Carmencita.

ESCAMILLO

Carmencita?

CARMEN

Carmen, Carmencita, as you like.

ESCAMILLO

Well then! Carmen or Carmencita, if I took it into my head to love you and be loved by you, what would you answer?

CARMEN

I should answer that you can love me just as you please, but as for being loved by me just at present, you mustn't think of it!

ESCAMILLO

Then I'll wait, and content myself with hoping . . .

CARMEN

It's not forbidden to wait, and it's always pleasant to hope.

ZUNIGA

quietly to Carmen

Ecoute-moi, Carmen, puisque tu ne veux pas venir avec nous, c'est moi qui dans une heure reviendrai ici . . .

CARMEN
Je ne vous conseille pas de revenir. . .

ZUNIGA

quietly to Carmen

Je reviendrai tout le même.

Out loud

Nous partons avec vous, torero, et nous nous joindrons au cortège qui vous accompagne.

Listen to me, Carmen. Since you won't come with us, it's I who'll come back here in an hour . . .

CARMEN
I don't advise you to come back . . .

ZUNIGA

I'll come back all the same.

We'll leave with you, torero, and tack ourselves on to the procession that accompanies you.

Everybody goes out except Carmen, Frasquita, Mercédès, and Lillas Pastia.

FRASQUITA *(à Pastia)*
Pourquoi étas-tu si pressé de les fair partir?

PASTIA
Le Dancaïre et Le Remendado viennent d'arriver . . .

PASTIA

opening a door and gesturing as he calls out

Les voici . . .

FRASQUITA *(to Pastia)*
Why were you so eager to send them away?

PASTIA
Dancaïro and Remendado have just arrived . . .

PASTIA

Here they are . . .

Enter Dancaïro and Remendado. Pastia closes the doors, puts up the shutters, etc., etc.

FRASQUITA
Eh bien, les nouvelles?

LE DANCAÏRE
Pas trop mauvaises, les nouvelles; nous arrivons de Gibraltar.

LE REMENDADO
Jolie ville, Gibraltar! . . . on y voit des Anglais, beaucoup d'Anglais, de jolis hommes les Anglais, un peu froids, mais distingués.

LE DANCAÏRE
Remendado! . . .

LE REMENDADO
Patron.

LE DANCAÏRE
Taisez-vous. Nous avons arrangé l'embarquement de marchandises anglaises. Nous irons les attendre près de la côte, nous en cacherons une partie dans la montagne et nous ferons passer le reste. Tous nos camarades ont été prévenus . . . mais c'est de vous trois surtout ue nous avons besoin . . .vous allez partir avec nous.

CARMEN (riant)
Pourquoi faire? Pour vous aider à porter des ballots?

LE REMENDADO
Oh! Non. . . faire porter des ballots à des dames . . . ça ne serait pas distingué.

FRASQUITA
Well, the news?

EL DANCAÏRO
Not too bad, the news. We've just come from Gibraltar.

EL REMENDADO
Nice town, Gibraltar! . . . you see the English there, lots of English, nice chaps the English, a trifle cold, but gentlemanly.

EL DANCAÏRO
Remendado! . . .

EL REMENDADO
Boss.

EL DANCAÏRO
Shut up. We are arranged to take on board some English goods. We're going to wait for it near the coast. We'll hide some of the stuff up the mountain and run the rest. All our comrades have been warned . . . but it's you three we need principally . . . you'll leave with us.

CARMEN (laughing)
What for? To help you carry the bales?

EL REMENDADO
Oh no!—make the ladies carry the bales . . . that wouldn't be at all the thing.

LE DANCAÏRE *(menaçant)*
Remendado?

EL DANCAÏRO *(threateningly)*
Remendado?

LE REMENDADO
Oui, patron.

EL REMENDADO
Yes, boss.

LE DANCAÏRE
Nous ne vous ferons pas porter de ballots, mais nous avons besoin de vous pour autre chose.

EL DANCAÏRO
We're not going to make you carry any bales, but we do need you for something else.

MARY GARDEN IN
THE ROLE OF CARMEN.

disc no. 1/track 20   *Nous avons en tête une affaire* (Quintet) The quintet is a fleet-footed miracle that, like Micaëla's scene with Don José in Act I, comes along like a cooling breeze to relieve all the erotic heat. It introduces outright comedy in the persons of the smugglers Dancaïro and Remendado who, with Frasquita and Mercédès, want Carmen to help them with a shipment of contraband. The men are bent on having the women flirt with the guards so the smugglers can slip past customs at the border. The heightened musical energy **(04:02)** of the quintet is an imaginative depiction of five sociopaths plotting their next bit of mischief.

LE DANCAÏRE
Nous avons en tête une affaire.

EL DANCAÏRO
We have a scheme in mind.

MERCÉDÈS ET FRASQUITA
Est-elle bonne, dites-nous?

MERCÉDÈS AND FRASQUITA
Tell us, is it good?

LE DANCAÏRE ET LE REMENDADO
Elle est admirable, ma chère;
mais nous avons besoin de vous.

EL DANCAÏRO AND EL REMENDADO
It's admirable, my dear;
but we require your services.

TOUS LE CINQ
De nous? etc.
De vous! etc.

QUINTET
Ours? etc.
Yours! etc.

LES DEUX HOMMES
Car nous l'avouons humblement,
et fort respectueusement;
quand il s'agit de tromperie,
de duperie, de volerie,
il est toujous bon, sur ma foi,
d'avoir les femmes avec soi.
Et sans elles,
mes toutes belles,
on ne fait jamais rien
de bien!

THE TWO MEN
For we humbly
and most respectfully acknowledge
when it's a question of trickery
of deception, of thieving,
it's always good, I swear,
to have women around.
And without them,
my lovelies,
no one ever does
any good!

LES TROIS FEMMES
Quoi! sans nous jamais rien
de bien?

LES DEUX HOMMES
N'êtes-vous pas de cet avis?

LES TROIS FEMMES
Si fait, je suis
de cet avis.
Si fait, vraiment je suis.

TOUS LES CINQ
Quand il s'agit de tromperie, etc.

LE DANCAÏRE
C'est dit alors; vous partirez?

FRASQUITA ET MERCÉDÈS
Quand vous voudrez.

LE DANCAÏRE
Mais tout de suite.

CARMEN
Ah! permettez!!
S'il vous plait de partir, partez,
mais je ne suis pas du voyage.
Je ne pars pas, je ne pars pas!

LES DEUX HOMMES
Carmen, mon amour, tu viendras—

CARMEN
Je ne pars pas; je ne pars pas!

THE THREE GIRLS
What? Without us no one does
any good?

THE TWO MEN
Isn't that your opinion?

GIRLS
Indeed, that's
my opinion.
Yes indeed, really it is.

QUINTET
When it's a question of trickery, etc.

EL DANCAÏRO
It's settled then; you'll go?

FRASQUITA AND MERCÉDÈS
Whenever you like.

EL DANCAÏRO
Why, straight away.

CARMEN
Ah! just a moment!
If you want to go, go;
but I'm not in on this trip.
I won't go! I won't go!

THE MEN
Carmen, my love, you will come—

CARMEN
I won't go! I won't go!

LES DEUX HOMMES
Et tu n'auras pas le courage
de nous laisser dans l'embarras.

FRASQUITA ET MERCÉDÈS
Ah! ma Carmen, tu viendras.

CARMEN
Je ne pars pas, etc.

LE DANCAÏRE
Mais, au moins la raison, Carmen,
tu la diras.

TOUS LES QUATRE
La raison, la raison!

CARMEN
Je la dirai certainement.

TOUS LES QUATRE
Voyons! Voyons!

CARMEN
La raison, c'est qu'en ce moment . . .

TOUS LES QUATRE
Eh bien? Eh bien?

CARMEN
Je suis amoureuse!

LES DEUX HOMMES (*stupéfaits*)
Qu'a-t-elle dit?

LES DEUX FEMMES
Elle dit qu'elle est amoureuse!

THE MEN
And you won't have the heart
to leave us in the lurch.

FRASQUITA AND MERCÉDÈS
Ah! My Carmen, you will come.

CARMEN
I won't go! etc.

EL DANCAÏRO
But the reason, Carmen,
at least you'll tell us the reason.

QUARTET
The reason, the reason!

CARMEN
Certainly I'll give it.

QUARTET
Let's have it! Let's have it!

CARMEN
The reason is that at this moment . . .

QUARTET
Well? Well?

CARMEN
I'm in love!

THE MEN (*astonished*)
What did she say?

THE GIRLS
She says she's in love!

TOUS LES QUATRE
Amoureuse!

CARMEN
Oui, amoureuse!

LE DANCAÏRE
Voyons, Carmen, sois sérieuse!

CARMEN
Amoureuse à perdre l'esprit!

LES DEUX HOMMES
La chose, certes, nous étonne,
mais ce n'est pas le premier jour
où vous aurez su, ma mignonne,
faire marcher de front le devoir et l'amour.

CARMEN
Mes amis, je serais fort aise
de partir avec vous ce soir;
mais cette fois ne vous déplaise,
il faudra que l'amour passe avant le devoir.

LE DANCAÏRE
Ce n'est pas là ton dernier mot?

CARMEN
Absolument!

LE REMENDADO
Il faut que tu te laisses attendrir.

TOUS LES QUATRE
Il faut venir, Carmen, il faut venir!
Pour notre affaire,
c'est nécessaire,

QUARTET
In love!

CARMEN
Yes, in love!

EL DANCAÏRO
See here, Carmen, be serious!

CARMEN
Head over heels in love!

THE MEN
This is certainly astonishing,
but it's not the first time,
my pet, that you've been able
to combine love and duty.

CARMEN
My friends, I'd be most happy
to go with you this evening;
but this time—don't be annoyed—
love must come before duty.

EL DANCAÏRO
That's not your final word?

CARMEN
Absolutely!

EL REMENDADO
You must relent.

QUARTET
You must come, Carmen, you must come!
It's necessary
for our scheme,

car entre nous . . .

for between ourselves . . .

CARMEN
Quant à cela, je l'admets avec vous . . .

CARMEN
As to that, I admit with you that . . .

RPRISE GÉNÉRALE
Quand il s'agit de tromperie, etc.

QUINTET (reprise)
When it's a question of trickery, etc.

LE DANCAÏRE
En voilà assez; je t'ai dit qu'il faillait venir et tu viendras . . . je suis le chef.

EL DANCAÏRO
Enough of that; I told you you must come, and you will come . . . I am the leader.

CARMEN
Comment dis-tu ça?

CARMEN
What's that you say?

LE DANCAÏRE
Je te dis que je suis le chef.

EL DANCAÏRO
I tell you I'm the leader.

CARMEN
Et tu crois que je t'obéirai?

CARMEN
And you think I'll obey you?

LE DANCAÏRE (furieux)
Carmen! . . .

EL DANCAÏRO (furious)
Carmen! . . .

LE REMENDADO

EL REMENDADO

throwing himself between Dancaïro and Carmen

Je vous en prie . . . des personnes si distinguées.

I beg you, such genteel persons.

LE DANCAÏRE
Amoureuse . . . ce n'est pas une raison, cela.

EL DANCAÏRO
In love . . . that's not a reason.

CARMEN
Partez sans moi . . . j'irai vous rejoindre demain, mais pour ce soir je reste.

CARMEN
Leave without me. I'll come and join you tomorrow, but for this evening I'm staying.

FRASQUITA

Je ne t'ai jamais vue comme cela; que attends-tu donc?

CARMEN

Un pauvre diable du soldat qui m'a rendu service . . .

MERCÉDÈS

Ce soldat qui était en prison?

CARMEN

Oui.

LE DANCAÏRE

Je parierais qu'il ne viendra pas.

CARMEN

Ne parie pas, tu perdrais . . .

FRASQUITA

I've never seen you like this. Who are you expecting?

CARMEN

A poor devil of a soldier who did me a service . . .

MERCÉDÈS

That soldier who was in prison?

CARMEN

Yes.

EL DANCAÏRO

I'd bet you he won't come.

CARMEN

Don't bet, you would lose . . .

José's voice is heard in the distance.

Scene Fifteen   **SONG**

JOSÉ

in the far distance

Halte là!
Qui va là?
Dragon d'Alcala!
Où t'en vas-tu par là,
Dragon d'Alcala?—
Moi, je m'en vais faire
mordre la poussière
à mon adversaire.—

JOSÉ

Halt!
Who goes there?
Dragoon of Alcala!
Where are you going there,
Dragoon of Alcala?—
Me, I'm going to make
my rival
bite the dust.—

S'il en est ainsi,
passez, mon ami.
Affaire d'honneur,
affaire de coeur;
pour nous tout est là
Dragons d'Alcala!

If that's the case,
pass, my friend.
An affair of honour,
an affair of the heart—
that explains everything for us
Dragoons of Alcala!

There is no break in the music. Carmen, Dancaïro, Remendado, Mercédès, and Frasquita watch the arrival of José through the half-open shutters.

MERCÉDÈS
C'est un dragon, ma foi.

MERCÉDÈS
Faith, it's a dragoon.

FRASQUITA
Un beau dragon.

FRASQUITA
A handsome dragoon.

LE DANCAÏRE *(à Carmen)*
Eh bien, Carmen, puisque tu ne veux venir que demain, sais-tu au moins ce que tu devrais faire?

EL DANCAÏRO *(to Carmen)*
Well, Carmen, since you won't come until tomorrow, d'you know at least what you ought to do?

CARMEN
Qu'est-ce que je devrais faire?

CARMEN
What is it I ought to do?

LE DANCAÏRE
Tu devrais décider ton dragon à venir avec toi et à se joindre à nous.

EL DANCAÏRO
You ought to persuade your dragoon to come with you and join us.

CARMEN
Ah! . . . si cela se pouvait! . . . Mais il n'y faut pas penser . . . ce sont des bêtises . . . il est trop niais.

CARMEN
Ah, if that were possible! . . . But you mustn't think of it . . . it's nonsense . . . he's too simple.

LE DANCAÏRE
Pourquoi l'aimes-tu puisque tu en conviens toi-même?

EL DANCAÏRO
Why do you love him, since you yourself admit it?

CARMEN
Parce qu'il est joli garçon donc et qu'il me plaît.

CARMEN
Because he's a nice boy and he pleases me.

LE REMENDADO *(avec fatuité)*
Le patron ne comprend pas ça, lui . . . qu'il suffise d'être joli garçon pour plaire aux femmes . . .

EL REMENDADO *(fatuously)*
The boss, he doesn't understand that . . . that it's enough to be a nice boy in order to please the women . . .

LE DANCAÏRE
Attends un peu, toi, attends un peu . . .

EL DANCAÏRO
Wait a moment, you, wait a moment . . .

Remendado makes his escape and goes out. Dancaïro pursues him and goes out in his turn, dragging along Mercédès and Frasquita who are trying to calm him down.

JOSÉ
Halte là!
Qui va là?
Dragon d'Alcala!
Où t'en vas-tu par là,
Dragon d'Alcala?—
Exact et fidèle,
je vais où m'appelle
l'amour de ma belle!—
S'il en est ainsi,
passez, mon ami.
Affaire d'honneur,
affaire de coeur,
pour nous tout est là,
Dragons d'Alcala!

JOSÉ
Halt!
Who goes there?
Dragoon of Alcala!
Where are you going there,
Dragoon of Alcala?—
Punctual and faithful,
I go where the love
of my fair lady calls me!—
If that's the case,
pass, friend.
An affair of honour,
an affair of the heart,
that explains everything for us
Dragoons of Alcala!

Don José enters.

CARMEN
Enfin . . . te voilà . . . C'est bien heureux!

CARMEN
At last . . . so there you are . . .this is a fine thing!

JOSÉ

Il y a deux heures seulement que je suis sorti de prison.

CARMEN

Qui t'empêchait de sortir plus tôt? Je t'avais envoyé une lime et une pièce d'or.

JOSÉ

Que veux-tu? J'ai encore mon honneur de soldat, et déserter me semblerait un grand crime . . Oh! Je ne t'en suis pas moins reconnaissant. La lime me servira pour affiler ma lance et je l'ai gardé comme souvenir de toi.

holding out the gold coin to her

Quant à l'argent . . .

CARMEN

Tiens, il l'a gardé!

shouting and hammering

Holà! . . . Lillas Pastia, holà!

enter Pastia

CARMEN

tossing him the coin

Apporte-nous du Manzanilla . . . apporte-nous de tout ce que tu as, de tout . . .

JOSÉ

It's only two hours since I came out of prison.

CARMEN

What prevented you from getting out sooner? I had sent you a file and a gold coin.

JOSÉ

What d'you expect? I still have my soldier's honour, and to desert would seem to be a great crime . . . Oh, I'm none the less grateful to you. The file will be useful to me for sharpening my lance and I've kept it as a memento of you.

as for the money . . .

CARMEN

Hullo, he's kept it!

Hi there! . . . Lillas Pastia, hi!

CARMEN

Bring us some Manzanilla . . . bring us everything you have, everything, the lot . . .

PASTIA
Tout de suite, mademoiselle Carmencita.

He goes out.

CARMEN *(à Don José)*
Tu regrettes d't être fait mettre en prison
pour mes beaux yeux?

JOSÉ
Non. On m'a mis en prison, on m'a ôté
mon grade, mais ça m'est égal.

CARMEN
Parce que tu m'aimes?

JOSÉ
Oui, parce que je t'aime, parce que je
t'adore.

CARMEN
Ton lieutenant était ici tour à l'heure, avec
d'autres officiers, ils nous ont fait danser.

JOSÉ
Tu as dansé?

CARMEN
Oui; et ton lieutenant s'est permis de me
dire qu'il m'adorait . . .

JOSÉ
Carmen!

CARMEN
Qu'est-ce que tu as? . . . Est-ce que tu serais
jaloux, par hasard?

PASTIA
At once, señorita Carmencita.

CARMEN *(to Don José)*
You regret having been put in prison for
the sake of my lovely eyes?

JOSÉ
No. They put me in prison, they stripped
me of my rank, but it's all one to me.

CARMEN
Because you love me?

JOSÉ
Yes, because I love you, because I adore
you.

CARMEN
Your lieutenant was here just now with
some other officers. They made us dance.

JOSÉ
You danced?

CARMEN
Yes; and your lieutenant allowed himself to
tell me that he adored me . . .

JOSÉ
Carmen!

CARMEN
What's the matter with you? . . . Would
you be jealous, by any chance?

JOSÉ
Mais certainement, je suis jaloux . . .

CARMEN
Eh bien, si tu le veux, je danserai pour toi maintenant, pour toi seul.

JOSÉ
Ah! que je t'aime, Carmen, que je t'aime!

CARMEN
Je l'espère bien.

JOSÉ
Why, certainly I'm jealous . . .

CARMEN
Well then, if you want me to, I'll dance for you now, for you alone.

JOSÉ
Ah, how I love you, Carmen, how I love you!

CARMEN
So I should hope.

SHIRLEY VERRETT
(B. 1931) MADE HER
METROPOLITAN OPERA
DEBUT IN THE TITLE
ROLE OF CARMEN.

Scene Sixteen   DUET

disc no. 2/track 1   *Je vais danser en votre honneur* Don José arrives, fresh from his stint in prison, and Carmen greets him with some teasing and a special treat she dances for him alone **(00:37)** in a way that suggests a tempestuous night of love is ahead for them. But Bizet brilliantly dramatizes the central conflict of the story in a few well-chosen strokes when he has Don José hear the reveille **(01:13)**. Carmen's explosive anger **(02:39)** when he tells her he must leave has an unsettling effect on Don José, whose psychotic reaction in the end is underlined by the return of the fate motive, heard in the opera's prelude.

CARMEN
Je vais danser en votre honneur,
et vous verrez, seigneur,
comment je sais moi-même accompagner
ma danse!
Mettez-vous là, Don José, je commence!

CARMEN
I am going to dance in your honour,
and you will see, my lord,
how I am able to accompany
my dance!
Sit down there, Don José, I'll begin!

She makes José sit down in a corner, and starts to dance, humming and accompanying herself with her castanets. José is entranced. Bugles are heard in the distance sounding Retreat. José cocks an ear. He comes over to Carmen and compels her to stop.

JOSÉ
Attendez, Carmen, rien qu'un moment,
arrête!

JOSÉ
Wait, Carmen, only for a moment,
stop!

CARMEN
Et pour quoi, s'il te plaît?

CARMEN
And why, if you please?

JOSÉ
Il me semble, là-bas . . .
oui, ce sont nos clairons que sonnent la
retraite!
Ne les entends-tu pas?

JOSÉ
I think, over there . . .
yes, those are our bugles sounding
Retreat!
Can't you hear them?

CARMEN

Bravo! Bravo! J'avais beau faire; il est
mélancholique de danser sans orchestre.
Et vive la musique
qui nous tombe du ciel!

CARMEN

Bravo! Bravo! I was trying in vain; it's dismal
dancing without an orchestra.
And long live music
that drops on us out of the skies!

She resumes her song. The bugles sound nearer, pass beneath the windows of the inn, then fade in the distance. José makes a new effort to tear himself from his contemplation of Carmen. He seizes her arm and compels her to stop once more.

JOSÉ

Tu ne m'as pas compris, Carmen, c'est la
retraite;
il faut que moi, je rentre au quartier pour
l'appel

JOSÉ

You didn't understand me, Carmen, it's
Retreat;
I've got to get back to quarters
for roll-call.

CARMEN

Au quartier! Pour l'appel!
Ah! j'étais vraiment trop bête!
Je me mettais en quartre
et je faisais des frais,
oui, je faisais des frais
pour amuser monsieur!
Je chantais! Je dansais!
Je crois, Dieu me pardonne,
qu'un peu plus, je l'aimais!
Taratata!
C'est le clarion qui sonne!
Taratata!
Il part! il est parti!
Va-t'en donc, canari!

CARMEN

To quarters! For roll-call!
Ah! Really I was too stupid!
I went out of my way
and took the trouble,
yes, I took the trouble
to entertain the gentleman!
I sang! I danced!
I believe, God forgive me,
I almost fell in love!
Taratata!
It's the bugle sounding!
Taratata!
He's off! He's gone!
Go on then, canary!*

angrily throwing his cap at him

*a reference to the yellow tunic of a Spanish dragoon.

Tiens; prends ton shako,
ton sabre, ta giberne;
et va-t'en, mon garçon, va-t'en!
Retourne à ta caserne!

JOSÉ
C'est mal à toi, Carmen, de te moquer de moi!
Je souffre de partir, car jamais, jamais
femme,
jamais femme avant toi,
aussi profoundemént n'avait troublé mon
âme!

CARMEN
"Taratata, mon Dieu! C'est la retraite!
Taratata, je vais être en retard!"
Il court, il perd la tête,
et voilà son amour!

JOSÉ
Ainsi, tu ne crois pas à mon amour?

CARMEN
Mais non!

JOSÉ
Eh bien! tu m'entendras!

CARMEN
Je ne veux rien entendre!

JOSÉ
Tu m'entendras!

CARMEN
Tu vas te faire attendre!

Here! Take your shako,
your sword, your bandolier;
and clear off, my son, clear off!
Clear off back to your barracks!

JOSÉ
It's cruel of you, Carmen, to make fun of me!
It pains me to go, for never, never has a
woman,
never before you has any woman
so deeply stirred my heart!

CARMEN
"Taratata, my God! It's the Retreat!
Taratata, I'm going to be late!"
He loses his wits, he rushes off,
and that's his love!

JOSÉ
So you don't believe in my love?

CARMEN
Of course not!

JOSÉ
Very well! You shall listen to me!

CARMEN
I won't listen to anything!

JOSÉ
You shall hear me!

CARMEN
You're going to be late!

JOSÉ
Tu m'entendras! Carmen!

CARMEN
Non! non! non! non!

JOSÉ
Oui, tu m'entendras!
Je le veux! Carmen,
tu m'entendras!

JOSÉ
You shall hear me! Carmen!

CARMEN
No! No! No! No!

JOSÉ
Yes, you shall hear me!
I insist! Carmen,
you shall hear me!

He reaches inside his tunic and takes out the acacia flower Carmen threw him in Act One.

disc no. 2/track 2 *La fleur que tu m'avais jetée* (Flower Song) The Flower Song is the tenor's big solo moment in Carmen, a beautiful aria that challenges the singer to deliver it with passion and, at the same time, a kind of neurotic tenderness. It is one of those arias with such beautiful surfaces that one does not have to look beneath them to appreciate it. Yet it is a disturbing moment in the context of the opera— a quality captured in Jon Vickers's performance on this recording—that ends with passionate declaration that rises **(03:19)** to an eerily soft high B-flat.

La fleur que tu m'avais jetée,
dans ma prison m'était restée.
Flétrie et sèche, cette fleur
gardait toujours sa douce odeur;
et pendant des heures entières,
sur mes yeux, fermant mes paupières,
de cette odeur je m'enivrais
et dans la nuit je te voyais!
Je me prenais à te maudire,
à te détester, à me dire
Pourquoi faut-it que le destin,
l'ait mise là sur mon chemin?

The flower that you threw to me
stayed with me in my prison.
Withered and dried up, that flower
always kept its sweet perfume;
and for hours at a time,
with my eyes closed,
I became drunk with its smell
and in the night I used to see you!
I took to cursing you,
detesting you, asking myself
why did destiny
have to throw her across my path?

Puis je m'accusais de blasphème,
et je ne sentais en moi-même,
je ne sentais qu'un seul désir,
un seul désir, un seul espoir
te revoir, ô Carmen, oui, te revoir!
Car tu n'avais eu qu'à paraître,
qu'à jeter un regard sur moi,
pour t'emparer de tour mon être,
ô ma Carmen!
et j'étais une chose à toi!
Carmen, je t'aime!

Then I accused myself of blasphemy,
and felt within myself,
I felt but one desire,
one desire, one hope
to see you again, Carmen, to see you again!
For you had only to appear,
only to throw a glance my way,
to take possession of my whole being,
O my Carmen,
and I was your chattel!
Carmen, I love you!

disc no. 2/track 3 *Non! tu ne m'aimes pas!* Carmen sees the potential for exploiting Don José's vulnerability and, in a rhythmically seductive phrase beginning with the words "Là-bas, là-bas . . ." **(00:19)**, she insists (much as she insisted in the Seguedille) that he join her and her smuggler friends.

CARMEN
Non, tu ne m'aimes pas!

CARMEN
No, you don't love me!

JOSÉ
Que dis-tu?

JOSÉ
What are you saying?

CARMEN
Non, tu ne m'aimes pas,
non! Car si tu m'aimais,
là-bas, là-bas,
tu me suivrais.

CARMEN
No, you don't love me,
no! For if you did,
you'd follow me over there.

JOSÉ
Carmen!

JOSÉ
Carmen!

CARMEN
Oui!—
Là-bas, là-bas, dans la montagne,

CARMEN
Yes!—
Away over there into the mountains,

JOSÉ
Carmen!

CARMEN
là-bas, là-bas, tu me suivrais.
Sur ton cheval tu me prendrais,
et comme un brave à travers la campagne,
en croupe, tu m'emporterais!
Là-bas, là-bas dans la montagne!

JOSÉ
Carmen!

CARMEN
Là-bas, là-bas, tu me suivrais,
Si tu m'aimais!
Tu n'y dépendrais de personne;
point d'officier à qui tu doives obéir
et point de retraite que sonne
pour dire à l'amoureux
qu'il est temps de partir!
Le ciel ouvert, la vie errante,
pour pays l'univers;
et pour loi ta volonté,
et surtout la chose enivrante
la liberté! la liberté!

JOSÉ
Mon Dieu!

CARMEN
Là-bas, là-bas dans la montagne,

JOSÉ
Carmen!

JOSÉ
Carmen!

CARMEN
away over there you'd follow me.
You'd take me up behind you on your
horse and like a daredevil you'd carry me
off across the country!
Way over there into the mountains!

JOSÉ
Carmen!

CARMEN
Away over there you'd follow me,
if you loved me!
There you'd not be dependent on anyone;
there'd be no officer you had to obey,
and no Retreat sounding
to tell a lover
that it is time to go!
The open sky, the wandering life,
the whole wide world your domain;
for law your own free will,
and above all, that intoxicating thing
Freedom! Freedom!

JOSÉ
Oh God!

CARMEN
Away over there into the mountains,

JOSÉ
Carmen!

CARMEN
là-bas, là-bas , si tu m'aimais,

JOSÉ
Tais-toi!

CARMEN
là-bas, là-bas tu me suivrais!
Sur ton cheval te me prendrais . . .

JOSÉ
Ah! Carmen! hélas! tais-toi!
tais-toi! mon Dieu!

CARMEN
et comme un brave, à travers la campagne,
oui, tu m'emporterais, si tu m'aimais.

JOSÉ
Hélas! hélas!

CARMEN
Oui, n'est-ce pas,
là-bas, là-bas tu me suivras,
tu m'aimes et tu me suivras!
Là-bas, là-bas emporte-moi!

JOSÉ
Pitié! Carmen! Pitié!
O mon Dieu, hélas!
Ah! Tais-toi! Tais-toi!
Non! Je ne veux plus t'écouter!
Quitter mon drapeau . . . déserter . . .
c'est la honte, c'est l'infamie!
Je n'en veux pas!

CARMEN
away over there, if you loved me,

JOSÉ
Stop it!

CARMEN
away over there you'd follow me!
You'd take me up on your horse . . .

JOSÉ
Ah, Carmen! Alas! Stop!
stop! Oh God!

CARMEN
and like a daredevil
you'd carry me off
across the country, if you loved me.

JOSÉ
Alas! Alas!

CARMEN
Yes, isn't it so,
you will follow me there,
you love me and you'll follow me!
Take me away over there!

JOSÉ
Pity, Carmen! Have pity!
Oh God, alas!
Ah, stop, stop!
No! I won't listen to you!
To abandon my colours . . . to desert . . .
that's shameful, that's dastardly!
I'll have none of it!

CARMEN Eh bien, pars!	**CARMEN** All right then, go!
JOSÉ Carmen, je t'en prie!	**JOSÉ** Carmen, I implore you!
CARMEN Non, je ne t'aime plus!	**CARMEN** No, I don't love you any more!
JOSÉ Ecoute!	**JOSÉ** Listen!
CARMEN Va! Je te hais! Adieu! Mais adieu pour jamais!	**CARMEN** Go! I hate you! Good-bye! And good-bye forever!
JOSÉ Eh bien, soit . . . adieu, adieu pour jamais!	**JOSÉ** All right, so be it . . . good-bye forever!
CARMEN Va-t'en!	**CARMEN** Get out!
JOSÉ Carmen! Adieu! Adieu pour jamais!	**JOSÉ** Carmen! Goodbye, good-bye forever!
CARMEN Adieu!	**CARMEN** Good-bye!

Don José hurries towards the door; just as he reaches it, somebody knocks.

Scene Seventeen   **FINALE**

disc no. 2/track 4   *Holà Carmen! Holà! Holà!* In the second-act finale, just as the smugglers arrive to collect Carmen, Zuniga blunders in, looking for Carmen. He is held captive, leaving Don José no recourse but to join the smugglers. The "Là-bas" melody **(03:51)** returns with militancy, for an entire band of smugglers is now gathering, transforming Carmen's insinuating siren song into a hymn to the rogue's life and bringing the act to an end.

ZUNIGA *(au dehors)* Holà! Carmen! Holà! Holà!	**ZUNIGA** *(outside)* Hallo there, Carmen! Hallo! Hallo!
JOSÉ Qui frappe? qui vient là?	**JOSÉ** Who's that knocking? Who's there?
CARMEN Tais-toi! Tais-toi!	**CARMEN** Keep quiet!
ZUNIGA	**ZUNIGA**

forcing the door

J'ouvre moi-même et j'entre.	I'm opening up myself, and coming in.

sees Don José—to Carmen

Ah! fi, ah! fi, la belle! Le choix n'est pas heureux; c'est se mésallier de prendre le soldat quand on a l'officier.	Ah! Fi, fi! My lovely lady! This isn't a happy choice; it's demeaning to take the soldier when you've got the officer.

to Don José

Allons! Décampe!	Off with you, get moving!
JOSÉ Non!	**JOSÉ** No!
ZUNIGA Si fait, tu partiras!	**ZUNIGA** You certainly will go!
JOSÉ Je ne partirai pas!	**JOSÉ** I shall not go!

ZUNIGA

striking him

Drôle!

JOSÉ

drawing his sword

Tonnerre! Il va pleuvoir des coups!

CARMEN

throwing herself between them

Au diable le jaloux! *(appelant)*
A moi! A moi!

Gypsies appear from all sides. Carmen points to Zuniga. Dancaïro and Remendado hurl themselves upon him and disarm him.

CARMEN
Bel officier! Bel officier, l'amour
vous joue en ce moment un assez vilain
tour.
Vous arrivez fort mal, hélas! Et nous
sommes forcés,
ne voulant être dénoncés,
de vous garder au moins . . . pendant une
heure.

LE DANCAÏRE ET LE REMENDADO
Mon chere monsieur,
nous allons, s'il vous plaît,
quitter cette demeure;
vous viendrez avec nous?

ZUNIGA

Scoundrel!

JOSÉ

By thunder! It's going to rain blows!

CARMEN

Devil take the jealous! *(calling)*
Help! Help!

CARMEN
My fine officer! My fine officer, love
at the moment is playing you a rather dirty
trick.
Your arrival is most untimely; and alas,
we are compelled,
not wishing to be betrayed, to detain you
. . . for at least an hour.

EL DANCAÏRO AND EL REMENDADO
My dear sir,
if you please, we are going to leave this
establishment;
you'll come with us?

CARMEN
C'est une promenade.

LE DANCAÏRE ET LE REMENDADO
Consentez-vous?

TOUS LES BOHÉMIENS
Répondez, camarade.

ZUNIGA
Certainement,
d'autant plus que votre argument
est un de ceux auxquels on ne résiste guère,
mais gare à vous! Gare à vous plus tard!

LE DANCAÏRE
La guerre, c'est la guerre!
En attendant, mon officier,
passez devant sans vous faire prier!

LE REMENDADO ET LES BOHÉMIENS
Passez devant sans vous faire prier!

The officer is led out by four gypsies armed with pistols.

CARMEN *(à Don José)*
Es-tu des nôtres maintenant?

JOSÉ
Il le faut bien.

CARMEN
Ah! Le mot n'est pas galant,
mais qu'importe, va, tu ty feras
quand tu verras
comme c'est beau, la vie errante;
pour pays, l'univers,

CARMEN
Just for a stroll.

EL DANCAÏRO AND EL REMENDADO
Do you consent?

ALL THE GYPSIES
Answer, comrade.

ZUNIGA
Certainly,
the more so since your argument
is one of those that can hardly be resisted;
but take care! Look out for yourselves later!

EL DANCAÏRO
War is war!
Meantime, my good sir,
carry on without further argument!

EL REMENDADO AND THE GYPSIES
Carry on without further argument!

CARMEN *(to Don José)*
Are you one of us now?

JOSÉ
I have no alternative.

CARMEN
Ah! that's not gallantly put,
but no matter, go, you'll take to it there
when you see
how fine is the wandering life;
the whole world your domain,

et pour loi ta volonté,
et surtout, la chose, enivrante
la liberté! La liberté!

Tous *(à Don José)*
Suis-nous à travers la campagne,
viens avec nous dans la montagnen,
suis-nous et tu t'y feras
quand tu verras, là-bas,
comme c'est beau, la vie errante;
pour pays, l'univers,
et pour loi, ta volonté!
Et surtout, la chose enivrante
la liberté! La liberté!
Le ciel ouvert, la vie errante,
pour pays tout l'univers;
pour loi ta volonté,
et surtout la chose enivrante:
la liberté, La liberté!

your own free will for law,
and above all that intoxicating thing
Freedom! Freedom!

All *(to Don José)*
Take to the country with us,
come with us into the mountains,
come with us and you'll take to it there
when you see, away over there;
how fine is the wandering life:
the whole world your domain,
your own free will for law!
And above all that intoxicating thing
Freedom! Freedom!
The open sky, the wandering life,
the whole wide world your domain;
your own free will for law,
and above all that intoxicating thing
Freedom! Freedom!

ENTR'ACTE

Act Three

Scene Eighteen

INTRODUCTION *The curtain rises on a wild and rocky scene; the night is dark and the solitude complete. During the musical prelude a smuggler appears at the top of the rocks, then another, then two more, and finally twenty here and there, climbing and scrambling over the rocks. Some of them are carrying heavy bales on their shoulders.*

disc no. 2/track 5

Entr'acte One of Bizet's most beautiful melodies appears in the entr'acte, apropos of nothing really—a soaring flute solo heard over arpeggios in the harp. The melody is never heard again but it effectively removes the audience from the bustle of Seville, placing the action in the country and perhaps reflecting Don José's sad reminiscence of happier times.

CHOEUR
Ecoute, écoute, compagnon, écoute,
la fortune est là-bas, là-bas,
mais prends garde pendant la route,
prends garde de faire un faux pas!

**LE DANCAÏRE, LE REMENDADO, JOSÉ,
CARMEN, MERCÉDÈS ET FRASQUITA**
Notre métier est bon,
mais pour le faire il faut
avoir une âme forte!
Et le péril est en haut, il est en bas,
il est partout, qu'importe!
Nous allons devant nous
sans souci du torrent,
san souci de l'orage,
san souci du soldat

CHORUS
Listen, friend, listen,
fortune lies over there,
but take care along the way,
and watch your step!

**EL DANCAÏRO, EL REMENDADO, JOSÉ,
CARMEN, MERCÉDÈS AND FRASQUITA**
Our calling is a good one,
but to follow it you must
have a stout heart!
There's danger up above, and down below,
it's everywhere—what of it!
We go forward
without worrying about the torrent,
without worrying abut the storm,
without worrying about the soldier

116

qui là-bas nous attend,
et nous guette au passage—
sans souci nous allons en avant!

Tous
Ecoute, compagnon, écoute, etc.

Le Dancaïre
Halte! Nous allons nous arrêter ici . . . ceux qui ont sommeil pourront dormir pendant une demi-heure.

Le Remendado

stretching himself out voluptuously

Ah!

Le Dancaïre
Je vais, moi, voir s'il y a moyen de faire entrer les marchandises dans la ville . . . une brèche s'est faite dans le mur d'enceinte et nous pourrions passer par là.

calling out

Remendado!

Le Remendado

waking up

Hé?

Le Dancaïre
Debout, tu vas venir avec moi.

who's waiting for us over there,
and keeping a sharp lookout for us—
we go forward without worrying!

All
Listen, friend, listen, etc.

El Dancaïro
Halt! We're going to stop here . . . those who feel sleepy can doss down for half an hour.

El Remendado

Ah!

El Dancaïro
Me, I'm going to see if there's some way of getting the stuff into the town . . . a gap has been made in the outer wall and we could get through that way.

Remendado!

El Remendado

Eh?

El Dancaïro
Get up, you're coming with me.

LE REMENDADO
Mais, patron . . .

LE DANCAÏRE
Qu'est-ce que c'est?

LE REMENDADO

getting up

Voilà, patron, voilà!

LE DANCAÏRE
Allons, passe devant.

LE REMENDADO
Et moi qui rêvais que j'allais pouvoir dormir
. . . C'était un rêve, hélas! c'était un rêve!

He goes out, followed by Dancaïro.
During this scene between Carmen and Don José, a few gypsy men light a fire, by
which Mercédès and Frasquita come and sit down; the others roll themselves up in
their cloaks, lie down and go to sleep.

JOSÉ
Voyons, Carmen . . . si je t'ai parlé trop dure-
ment, je t'en demande pardon faisons la paix.

CARMEN
Non.

JOSÉ
Tu es le diable, Carmen?

CARMEN
Oui, qu'est-ce que tu regardes là, à quoi
penses-tu?

EL REMENDADO
But, boss . . .

EL DANCAÏRO
What's that?

EL REMENDADO

Here we are, boss, here!

EL DANCAÏRO
Right, go on ahead.

EL REMENDADO
And I who thought I was going to be able to
sleep . . . It was a dream, alas, it was a dream!

JOSÉ
Look, Carmen . . . if I spoke to you too
harshly, I ask your forgiveness. Let's make up.

CARMEN
No.

JOSÉ
You're worried, Carmen?

CARMEN
Yes, what's that you're looking at there,
what are you thinking of?

JOSÉ
Je me dis que là-bas il y a une bonne vieille femme qui croit que je suis encore un honnête homme . . .

CARMEN
Une bonne vieille femme?

JOSÉ
Oui; ma mère.

CARMEN
Ta mère. Eh bien, tu ne ferais pas mal d'aller la retrouver.

JOSÉ
Carmen, si tu me parles encore de nous séparer . . .

CARMEN
Tu me tuerais, peut-être?

José does not answer

JOSÉ
I'm telling myself that down there is a good old woman who believes me still to be an honest man . . .

CARMEN
A good old woman?

JOSÉ
Yes, my mother.

CARMEN
Your mother. Well then, you'd do no harm by going to find her.

JOSÉ
Carmen, if you talk to me any more about us separating . . .

CARMEN
You would kill me, perhaps?

disc no. 2/track 8 *A la bonne heure . . . Mêlons! Coupons!* (Card Trio) This is the moment that, for Carmen, is the crux of the action in the opera. Frasquita and Mercédès are playing with tarot cards. When Carmen tries her hand, the cards reveal her dire fate **(03:27)** She is hurtling toward death, and there is nothing she can do about it. She is devastated and almost instantly resigned to what seems inevitable. The section of the scene beginning with "En vain pour éviter les réponses amères" **(04:05)** reveals her fatalistic attitude in a mournful melody that develops with the same staggering intensity as the fate motive. It is perhaps the most substantial and beautiful solo moment Carmen has in the entire opera.

CARMEN
A la bonne heure . . . J'ai vu dans les cartes que nous devions finir ensemble.

CARMEN
Well and good . . . I've seen in the cards that we are to finish together.

JOSÉ
Tu es le diable, Carmen?

JOSÉ
You're worried, Carmen?

CARMEN
Mais oui, je te l'ai déjà dit . . .

CARMEN
Why yes, I've already told you so . . .

Scene Nineteen   **TRIO**   *She turns her back on José and goes and sits down by Mercédès and Frasquita. After a moment of indecision, Don José moves off in his turn and goes and stretches himself out upon the rocks. During the final exchanges in the foregoing scene, Mercédès and Frasquita have been spreading out playing cards in front of them.*

FRASQUITA ET MERCÉDÈS
Mêlons! Coupons!
Bien, c'est cela!
Trois cartes ici . . .
Quatre là!
Et maintenant, parlez, mes belles,
de l'avenir, donnez-nous des nouvelles;
dites-nous qui nous trahira,
dites-nous qui nous aimera!
Parlez, parlez!

FRASQUITA AND MERCÉDÈS
Shuffle! Cut!
Good, that's that!
Three cards here . . .
four there!
And now speak, my lovelies,
give us news of the future;
tell us who's going to betray us,
tell us who's going to love us!
Speak! Speak!

FRASQUITA
Moi, je vois un jeune amoureux,
qui m'aime on ne peut davantage.

FRASQUITA
Me, I see a young suitor,
no one could love me more.

MERCÉDÈS
Les mien est très riche et très vieux,
mais il parle de mariage.

MERCÉDÈS
Mine is very rich and very old,
but he talks of marriage.

FRASQUITA
Je me campe sur son cheval,
et dans la montagne il m'entraîne.

FRASQUITA
I settle myself firmly on his horse
and he carries me off into the mountains.

MERCÉDÈS
Dans un château presque royal,
le mien m'installe en souveraine!

FRASQUITA
De l'amour à n'en plus finir,
tous les jours, nouvelles folies!

MERCÉDÈS
De l'or tant, que j'en puis tenir,
des diamants, des pierreries!

FRASQUITA
Le mien devient un chef fameux,
cent hommes marchent à sa suite!

MERCÉDÈS
Le mien en croirai-je mes yeux?
Oui . . . il meurt!
Ah! je suis veuve et j'hérite!

REPRISE DE L'ENSEMBLE
Parlez encor, parlez, mes belles, etc.

MERCÉDÈS
In an almost royal castle
mine installs me in queenly state!

FRASQUITA
Never-ending love,
every day new raptures!

MERCÉDÈS
As much gold as I can take,
diamonds, precious stones!

FRASQUITA
Mine becomes a famous leader,
a hundred men march in his train!

MERCÉDÈS
Mine . . . can I believe my eyes?
Yes . . . he dies
Ah! I'm a widow and I inherit!

TOGETHER REPRISE
Speak again, speak, my lovelies, etc.

They begin to consult the cards again.

MERCÉDÈS
Fortune!

FRASQUITA
Amour!

CARMEN
Voyons, que j'essaie à mon tour.

MERCÉDÈS
Fortune!

FRASQUITA
Love!

CARMEN
Let's see—let me have a try.

She starts to turn up the cards.

Carreau, pique . . . la mort!
J'ai bien lu . . . moi d'abord.
Ensuite lui . . . pour tous les deux la mort!

Diamond, spade . . . Death!
I read it clearly . . . me first.
Then him . . . for both of us, Death!

in a low voice, while continuing to shuffle the cards

En vain pour éviter les réponses amères,
en vain tu mêleras;
cela ne sert à rien, les cartes
sont sincères et ne mentiront pas!
Dans le livre d'en haut
si ta page est heureuse,
mêle et coupe sans peur,
la carte sous tes doigts se tournera joyeuse,
t'annonçant le bonheur.
Mais si tu dois mourir,
si le mot redoutable
est écrit par le sort,
recommence vingt fois, la carte impitoyable
répétera la mort!

In vain to avoid bitter replies,
in vain will you shuffle;
that achieves nothing, the cards
are truthful and will not lie!
If your page in the book
up above is a happy one,
shuffle and cut without fear,
the card under your fingers will turn up
nicely, foretelling good luck.
But if you are to die,
if the terrible word
has been written by Destiny,
begin twenty times—the pitiless card
will repeat Death!

turning up the cards

Encor! Encor! Toujours la mort!

Again! Always Death!

FRASQUITA ET MERCÉDÈS
Parlez encor, parlez mes belles, etc.

FRASQUITA AND MERCÉDÈS
Speak again, my lovelies, speak! etc.

CARMEN
Encore! le désepoir!
Toujours la mort!

CARMEN
Again! Despair!
Always Death!

Dancaïro and Remendado return

CARMEN
Eh bien? . . .

CARMEN
Well? . . .

LE DANCAÏRE Eh bien, j'avais raison de ne pas me fier de Lillas Pastia. Nous avons aperçu trois douaniers qui gardaient la brèche.	**EL DANCAÏRO** Well, I was right not to trust Lillas Pastia. We spotted three customs men guarding the gap.
CARMEN *(en riant)* N'ayez pas peur, Dancaïre, nous vous en répondrons de vos trois douaniers . . .	**CARMEN** *(laughing)* Have no fear, Dancaïro, we'll take care of your three customs men for you . . .
JOSÉ *(furieux)* Carmen!	**JOSÉ** *(furious)* Carmen!
LE DANCAÏRE Ah! tu vas nous laisser tranquilles avec ta jalousie. Tu vas te placer là, sur cette hauteur. Dans le cas où tu apercevrais quelqu'un, passes ta colère sur l'indiscret. En route alors . . .	**EL DANCAÏRO** Ah, you will give us a rest from your jealousy. You will post yourself there on that height. If you should happen to spot anyone, take your anger out on such an ill-advised person. On our way, then . . .

to the women

Mais vous me répondrez vraiment de ces trois douaniers?	But you really will answer to me for these three customs men?
CARMEN N'ayez pas peur, Dancaïre.	**CARMEN** Have no fear, Dancaïro.

 ENSEMBLE WITH CHORUS

CARMEN, MERCÉDÈS ET FRASQUITA Quant au douanier, c'est notre affaire, tout comme un autre il aime à plaire, il aime à faire le galant; ah! laissez-nous passer en avant!	**CARMEN, MERCÉDÈS AND FRASQUITA** As for the customs man, he's our affair; just like the next man he loves to please, he loves to play the gallant; ah! leave us to go on ahead!

TOUTES LES FEMMES
Quant au douanier, c'est notre affaire, etc.

TOUS
Il aime à plaire!

MERCÉDÈS
Le douanier sera clément!

TOUS
Il est galant!

CARMEN
Le douanier sera charmant!

TOUS
Il aime à plaire!

MERCÉDÈS
Le douanier sera galant!

FRASQUITA
Oui, le douanier sera même entreprenant!

TOUS
Oui, le douanier c'est notre/leur affaire,
tout comme un autre il aime à plaire,
il aime à faire le galant,
laissez-nous/les passer en avant!

CARMEN, MERCÉDÈS ET FRASQUITA
Il ne s'agit plus de bataille,
non, il s'agit tout simplement
de se laisser prendre la taille
et d'écouter un compliment.
S'il faut aller jusqu'au sourire,
que voulez-vous, on sourira!

ALL THE GIRLS
As for the customs man, he's our affair, etc.

EVERYONE
He loves to please!

MERCÉDÈS
The customs man will be easy on us!

EVERYONE
He is gallant!

CARMEN
The customs man will be charming!

ALL
He loves to please!

MERCÉDÈS
The customs man will be gallant!

FRASQUITA
Yes, the customs man will even be forward!

ALL
Yes, the customs man is our/their affair;
just like the next man he loves to please,
he loves to play the gallant;
let us/them go on ahead!

CARMEN, MERCÉDÈS AND FRASQUITA
It's no longer a question of battle;
no, it's simply a question
of letting ourselves be taken by the waist
and listening to a compliment.
If it's necessary to go as far as a smile,
what of it?—we'll smile!

TOUTES LES FEMMES
Et d'avance, je puis le dire,
la contrebande passera!
En avant! Marchons! Allons!

TOUT LE MONDE
Oui, le douanier c'est notre/leur affaire, etc.

ALL THE WOMEN
And here and now I can say
the stuff will get through!
Forward! On our way! Let's go!

ALL
Yes, the customs man is our/their affair, etc.

Everyone leaves, Don José brings up the rear, examining the priming of his carbine; just before he disappears, a man is seen moving behind a rock. It is Micaëla's guide. The guide advances cautiously, then signals to Micaëla that the coast is clear.

LE GUIDE
Nous y sommes.

MICAËLA

entering

C'est ici.

LE GUIDE
Oui, vilain endroit, n'est-ce pas, et pas rassurant du tout?

MICAËLA
Je ne vois personne.

LE GUIDE
Ils reviendront bientôt. Ils n'ont pas emporté toutes leurs marchandises . . . prenez garde . . . l'un de leurs doit être en sentinelle et si l'on nous apercevrait . . .

MICAËLA
Je l'espère bien qu'on m'apercevra . . . puisque je suis venue ici justement pour

THE GUIDE
We're there.

MICAËLA

This is the place.

THE GUIDE
Yes, nasty spot, isn't it, and not at all reassuring?

MICAËLA
I don't see anybody.

THE GUIDE
They'll come back soon, for they haven't taken away all their goods . . . take care . . . one of their men must be on sentry–go, and if we were seen . . .

MICAËLA
I sincerely hope someone *will* see me . . . since that's just what I've come here for, to

parler à un de ces contrebandiers . . .

LE GUIDE
Eh bien, vous pouvez vous vanter d'avoir
du courage . . . venir ainsi affronter ces
Bohémiens . . .

MICAËLA
Je n'aurais pas peur, je vous assure.

LE GUIDE
Bien vrai?

MICAËLA
Bien vrai.

LE GUIDE (*naïvement*)
Alors je vous demanderai la permission de
m'en aller. Si ça ne vous fait rien, j'irai vous
attendre à l'auberge au bas de la montagne.
Vous restez décidément?

THE GUIDE
Well now, you can boast of having courage
. . . to come here like this to face these gypsies . . .

MICAËLA
I shouldn't be afraid, I assure you.

THE GUIDE
Truly?

MICAËLA
Truly.

THE GUIDE (*naïvely*)
Then I'll ask your permission to take
myself off. If it's all the same to you I'll go
and wait for you in the inn at the foot of
the mountain.
You're determined to stay?

disc no. 2/track 11 *Oui, je reste! . . . Je dis que rien ne m'épouvante* (Micaëla's Air) At this
depressing point in the opera, the air Bizet wrote for Micaëla is always welcome.
It is an elegant, glowing testament to her faith in her love for Don José **(00:27)**.
Like the first-act duet, it would not be out of place in an opera of Gounod or
Massenet. The orchestration is particularly effective, with the melody borne on
swirling arpeggios in the cellos, as if to suggest the uncertainty that surrounds
her unshakable fidelity to her beloved.

MICAËLA
Oui, je reste!

LE GUIDE
Que tous les saints du paradis vous soient

MICAËLA
Yes, I'm staying!

THE GUIDE
May all the saints in paradise come to your

en aide alors, mais c'est une drôle idée que vous avez là . . .

MICAËLA

looking around her

Mon guide avait raison . . . l'edroit n'est pas bien rassurant.

aid then, but it's a funny idea you've got there . . .

MICAËLA

My guide was right . . . it's not a very reassuring spot.

HILDE GUEDEN, AN AUSTRIAN LYRIC SOPRANO, AS MICAËLA.

Scene Twenty-One **AIR**

MICAËLA
Je dis, que rien ne m'épouvante,
je dis, hélas! que je réponds de moi;
mais j'ai beau faire la vaillante,
au fond du coeur, je meurs d'effroi!
Seule en ce lieu sauvage,
toute seule j'ai peur,
mais j'ai tort d'avoir peur;
vous me donnerez du courage,
vous me protégerez, Seigneur.

MICAËLA
I say that nothing frightens me, I say, alas,
that I have only myself to depend on;
but I have tried in vain to be brave,
at heart I'm dying of fright!
Alone in this wild place,
all alone, I'm afraid,
but I do wrong to be afraid;
you will give me courage
you will protect me, Lord.

Je vais voir de près cette femme
dont les artifices maudits
ont fini par faire un infâme
de celui que j'amais jadis
elle est dangereuse, elle est belle,
mais je ne veux pas avoir peur,
je parlerai haut devant elle.
Ah! Seigneur,
vous me protégerez!
Ah! je dis, que rien ne m'épouvante, etc.
. . . protégez-moi, O Seigneur,
Protégez-moi, Seigneur!
Mais . . . je ne me trompe pas . . . sur ce
rocher, c'est Don José.

I shall get a close look at this woman
whose evil wiles
have finished by making a criminal
of the man I once loved
she is dangerous, she is beautiful,
but I won't be afraid,
I shall speak out in front of her,
Ah! Lord,
you will protect me!
Ah! I say that nothing will frighten me, etc.
. . . protect me, O Lord,
protect me, Lord!
But. . . I'm not mistaken . . . on that
rock—it's Don José.

calling out

José! José!

José! José!

Terrified

disc no. 2/track 12 *Mais . . . je ne me trompe pas* Micaëla hides when she sees Don José fire his gun at a figure who turns out to be Escamillo. The air is thick with testosterone in the vigorous duet that follows **(00:34)**, in which Don José boldly challenges the man he sees as his rival while Escamillo—obviously a far more skilled fighter—is amused by his passion. Though the second half of the duet is often cut, it is heard in its entirety here **(02:23)**, revealing that Escamillo spares Don José's life when he has the better of him, even though Don José was ready to kill him.

Mais que fait-il? . . . Il arme sa carabine, il
ajuste . . . il fait feu.

But what is he doing? . . . He's cocking his
carbine . . . he's aiming . . . he fires.

A shot is heard.

Ah! mon Dieu, j'ai trop présumé de mon
courage . . .

Ah, my God, I overestimated my courage . . .

She disappears behind the rocks. At the same moment Escamillo comes in, holding his hat in his hand.

ESCAMILLO
Quelques lignes plus bas, et ce n'est pas moi qui aurais le plaisir de combattre les taureaux que je suis en train de conduire . . .

Enter José

JOSÉ

carrying his cloak

Qui êtes-vous? Répondez.

ESCAMILLO

very calm

Eh là . . . doucement!

Scene Twenty-Two **DUET**

ESCAMILLO
Je suis Escamillo, Torero de Grenade!

JOSÉ
Escamillo!

ESCAMILLO
C'est moi!

JOSÉ

ESCAMILLO
A little lower . . . and it isn't I who would have the pleasure of fighting the bulls I'm about to drive . . .

JOSÉ

Who are you? Answer.

ESCAMILLO

Eh eh . . . gently!

ESCAMILLO
I'm Escamillo, the Granada matador!

JOSÉ
Escamillo!

ESCAMILLO
That's me!

JOSÉ

Je connais votre nom,
soyez le bienvenu; mais vraiment, camarade,
vous pouviez y rester.

ESCAMILLO
Je ne vous dis pas non,
mais je suis amoureux, mon cher, à la folie,
et celui-là serait un pauvre compagnon,
qui, pour voir ses amours, ne risquerait sa vie!

JOSÉ
Celle que vous aimez est ici?

ESCAMILLO
Justement.
C'est une zingara, mon cher.

JOSÉ
Elle s'appelle?

ESCAMILLO
Carmen.

JOSÉ
Carmen!

ESCAMILLO
Carmen! oui, mon cher.
Elle avait pour amant
un soldat qui a déserté pour elle.
Ils s'adoraient, mais c'est fini, je crois.
Les amours de Carmen ne durent pas six mois.

JOSÉ
Vous l'aimez cependant!

I know your name,
you're welcome; but truly, comrade,
that could have been the end of you.

ESCAMILLO
I'm not denying it, but, my friend, I am
madly in love,
and he would be a wretched fellow
who wouldn't risk his live to see his ladylove!

JOSÉ
The girl you love is here?

ESCAMILLO
Exactly.
She's gypsy girl, my friend.

JOSÉ
Her name?

ESCAMILLO
Carmen.

JOSÉ
Carmen!

ESCAMILLO
Carmen! Yes, my friend.
She had as a lover
a soldier who once deserted on her account.
They adored each other, but it's over, I think.
Carmen's affairs don't last six months.

JOSÉ
Yet you love her!

ESCAMILLO
Je l'aime!
Oui, mon cher, je l'aime à la folie!

JOSÉ
Mais pour nous enlever nos filles de bohème,
savez-vous bien qu'il faut payer?

ESCAMILLO
Soit! On paiera.

JOSÉ
Et que le prix se paie à coups de navaja!

ESCAMILLO
A coups de navaja!

JOSÉ
Comprenez-vous?

ESCAMILLO
Le discours est très net.
Ce déserteur, ce beau soldat qu'elle aime,
ou du moins qu'elle aimait—
c'est donc vous?

JOSÉ
Oui, c'est moi-même!

ESCAMILLO
J'en suis ravi, mon cher,
et le tour est complet!

ESCAMILLO
I love her!
Yes, my friend, I love her to distraction!

JOSÉ
But to take our gypsy girls away from us
you know that you have to pay?

ESCAMILLO
All right! I'll pay.

JOSÉ
And that the price is paid with the knife!

ESCAMILLO
With the knife!

JOSÉ
You understand?

ESCAMILLO
You put it very clearly.
This deserter, this fine soldier she loves,
or rather, used to love—
is you, then?

JOSÉ
Yes, myself!

ESCAMILLO
I'm delighted, my friend,
and the wheel's come full circle!

Both draw their knives and wrap their left arm in their cloaks.

JOSÉ
Enfin ma colère

JOSÉ
At last my rage has found an outlet!

trouve à qui parler!
Le sang, je l'espère,
va bientôt couler, etc.

Blood, I hope,
will soon flow, etc.

ESCAMILLO
Quelle maladresse,
j'en rirais vraiment!
Chercher la maîtresse
et trouver l'amant! etc.

ESCAMILLO
What a predicament,
I could laugh at it, really!
To look for the mistress
and find the lover! etc.

ENSEMBLE
Mettez-vous en garde,
et veillez sur vous!
Tant pis pour qui tarde
à parer les coups!
En garde! Allons! Veillez sur vous!

TOGETHER
Put up your guard,
and look out for yourself!
So much the worse for the one
who's slow at parrying!
On guard! Come on! Look out for yourself!

They take up positions on guard at some distance from each other.

ESCAMILLO
Je la connais, ta garde navarraise.
Et je te previens en ami,
Qu'elle ne vaut rien . . .

ESCAMILLO
I know it, your Navarrais-style guard,
and I warn you, in a friendly way,
that it's no good . . .

Without answering, Don José advances upon the matador.

A ton aise.
Je t'aurai du moins averti.

As you like.
At least I'll have warned you.

Fight. Incidental music. The matador, very calm, attempts only to defend himself.

JOSÉ
Tu m'épargnes, maudit.

JOSÉ
You're not trying, you devil.

ESCAMILLO
A ce jeu de couteau
je suis trop fort pour toi.

ESCAMILLO
At this knife-play
I'm too good for you.

JOSÉ
Voyons cela.

JOSÉ
Let's see.

A swift and very lively hand-to-hand engagement. Don José finds himself at the mercy of the matador, who does not strike.

ESCAMILLO
Tout beau,
Ta vie est à moi, mais en somme
j'ai pour métier de frapper le taureau,
Non de trouer le coeur de l'homme.

ESCAMILLO
Steady,
your life belongs to me, but in short
my job is to kill bulls,
not to bore holes in men's hearts.

JOSÉ
Frappe ou bien meurs . . . Ceci n'est pas un jeu.

JOSÉ
Strike, or die . . . this isn't a game.

ESCAMILLO

disengaging himself

Soit, mais au moins respire un peu.

ESCAMILLO

All right, but at least get your breath.

Reprise of ensemble

JOSÉ
Enfin ma colère
trouve à qui parler etc.

JOSÉ
At last my rage
has found an outlet, etc.

ESCAMILLO
Quelle maladresse,
j'en rirais vraiment! etc.

ESCAMILLO
What a predicament,
I could laugh at it, really! etc.

CARMEN
Holà, holà! José!

ESCAMILLO
Vrai, j'ai l'âme ravie
que ce soit vous, Carmen, que me sauviez
la vie!
(à Don José)
Quant à toi, beau soldat,
je prendrai ma revanche,
et nous jouerons la belle,
le jour où tu voudras reprendre le combat!

LE DANCAÏRE
C'est bon, c'est bon, plus querelle!
Nous, nous allons partir.

to Escamillo

Et toi, l'ami, bonsoir!

ESCAMILLO
Souffrez au moins qu'avant de vous dire au
revoir, je vous invite tous aux courses de
Séville. Je compte pour ma part y briller de
mon mieux
et qui m'aime y viendra!

to José, who makes a threatening gesture

L'ami, tiens-toi tranquille,
j'ai tout dit et je n'ai plus ici
qu'à faire mes adieux!

CARMEN
Stop, stop, José!

ESCAMILLO
Really, I'm overjoyed
that it should be you, Carmen, who saved
my life!
(to Don José)
As for you, my fine soldier,
I'll take my revenge,
and we'll play for two out of three
whenever you wish to renew the fight!

EL DANCAÏRO
Enough, enough, no more quarreling!
We must get going.

And you, my friend, good night!

ESCAMILLO
Allow me at least, before I say goodbye,
to invite you all to the bullfights at Seville.
I expect to be at my most brilliant there,
and who loves me will come!

Friend, keep calm,
I've had my say, and I've nothing more
to do here but make my farewells!

Leisurely exit of Escamillo. Don José tries to attack him but is held back by Dancaïro and Remendado.

JOSÉ *(à Carmen)*
Prends garde à toi, Carmen, je suis las de souffrir!

JOSÉ *(to Carmen)*
Take care, Carmen, I'm weary of suffering!

Carmen answers him with a slight shrug of her shoulders and walks off.

LE DANCAÏRE
En route, en route, il faut partir!

EL DANCAÏRO
Let's get going! We must be off!

TOUS
En route, en route, il faut partir!

ALL
Let's get going! We must be off!

LE REMENDADO
Halte! quelqu'un est là qui cherche à se cacher.
He brings in Micaëla.

EL REMENDADO
Stop! There's someone there trying to hide!

CARMEN
Une femme!

CARMEN
A woman!

LE DANCAÏRE
Pardieu, la surprise est heureuse!

EL DANCAÏRO
Lord, a pleasant surprise!

JOSÉ
Micaëla!

JOSÉ
Micaëla!

MICAËLA
Don José!

MICAËLA
Don José!

JOSÉ
Malheureuse!
Que viens-tu faire ici?

JOSÉ
Poor girl!
What are you doing here?

MICAËLA
Moi, je viens te chercher.

MICAËLA
I've come looking for you.

Là-bas est la chaumière,
où sans cesse priant
une mère, ta mère,
pleure, hélas sur son enfant.
Elle pleure et t'appelle,
elle pleure et te tend les bras;
tu prendras pitié d'elle,
José, ah! José, tu me suivras!

CARMEN
Va-t'en! Va-t'en! Tu feras bien,
notre métier ne te vaut rien!

JOSÉ
Tu me dis de la suivre?

CARMEN
Oui, tu devrais partir!

JOSÉ
Tu me dis de la suivre
pour que toi, tu puisses courir
après ton nouvel amant!
Non! non vraiment!
Dût-il m'en coûter la vie,
non, Carmen, je ne partirai pas,
et la chaîne qui nous lie
nous liera jusqu'au trépas!
Dût-il m'en coûter la vie, etc.

MICAËLA
Ecoute-moi, je t'en prie,
ta mère te tend les bras,
cette chaîne que te lie,
José, tu la briseras!

Down there is the cottage
where, praying unceasingly,
a mother, your mother,
weeps, alas, for her son.
She weeps and calls you,
she weeps and holds out her arms to you;
you will take pity on her,
José, ah José, you will come with me!

CARMEN
Go on! Go on! You'll do well to go;
our business means nothing to you!

JOSÉ
You're telling me to go with her?

CARMEN
Yes, you ought to go!

JOSÉ
You're telling me to go with her
so that you can run after
your new lover!
No! Not likely!
Though it should cost me my life,
no, Carmen, I shall not go away,
and the bond which unites us
shall unite us till death!
Though it should cost me my life, etc.

MICAËLA
Listen to me, I implore you,
your mother holds out her arms to you,
that bond which unites you,
José, you will break it!

FRASQUITA, MERCÉDÈS, REMENDADO, DANCAÏRE, CHOEUR
Il t'en coûtera la vie,
José, si tu ne pars pas,
et la chaîne qui vous lie
se rompra par ton trépas.

JOSÉ *(à Micaëla)*
Laisse-moi!

MICAËLA
Hélas, José!

JOSÉ
Car je suis condamné!

FRASQUITA, MERCÉDÈS, REMENDADO, DANCAÏRE, CHOEUR
José! Prends garde!

JOSÉ *(à Carmen)*
Ah! je te tiens, fille damnée,
je te tiens, et je te forcerai bien
à subir la destinée
qui rive ton sort au mien!
Dût-il m'en coûter la vie,
non, non, non, je ne partirai pas!

CHOEUR
Ah! prends garde, prends garde, Don José!

MICAËLA
Une parole encor, ce sera la dernière.
Hélas! José, ta mère se meurt, et ta mère
ne voudrait pas mourir sans t'avoir pardon-
né.

FRASQUITA, MERCÉDÈS, REMENDADO, DANCAÏRO, CHORUS
It will cost you your life,
José, if you don't go,
and the bond which unites you
will be broken by your death.

JOSÉ *(to Micaëla)*
Leave me!

MICAËLA
Alas, José!

JOSÉ
For I am doomed!

FRASQUITA, MERCÉDÈS, REMENDADO, DANCAÏRO, CHORUS
José! Take care!

JOSÉ *(to Carmen)*
Ah! I've got you, accursed girl,
I've got you, and I shall compel you
to bow to the destiny
that links your fate with mine!
Though it should cost me my life,
no, no, no, I shall not go!

CHORUS
Ah! Take care, take care, Don José!

MICAËLA
One word more, this will be the last.
Alas! José, your mother is dying, and she
doesn't want to die without having forgiven
you.

JOSÉ
Ma mère! Elle se meurt?

MICAËLA
Oui, Don José.

JOSÉ
Partons, ah, partons!
(à Carmen) Sois contente, je pars, mais nous
nous reverrons!

He hurries off with Micaëla.

ESCAMILLO *(au loin)*
Toréador, en guarde! etc.

Don José stops at the back, on the rocks. He hesitates, but, after a moment, goes on his way with Micaëla. Carmen rushes in the direction of the voice. The gypsies take up their bales and prepare to leave.

JOSÉ
My mother! She's dying?

MICAËLA
Yes, Don José.

JOSÉ
Let's go, ah, let's go! *(to Carmen)*
Be satisfied! I'm going, but we shall meet
again!

ESCAMILLO *(in the distance)*
Toreador, on guard! etc.

Act Four

Scene Twenty-four **CHORUS** ∞ *A square in Seville, with the walls of the old arena in the back-ground. The entrance to the ring is closed by a long curtain. A bullfight is about to take place, and there is great excitement. Hawkers move about offering water, oranges, fans, etc.*

disc no. 2/track 14 *Entr'acte* The dramatic and flavorful introduction to the last act places the action squarely back in the city, amid the excitement before a bullfight. The darting, dancing rhythms and the unpredictable flair of the orchestration suggest vivid images that will appear when the curtain rises.

CHOEUR
A deux cuartos! A deux cuartos!
Des éventails pour s'éventer!
Des oranges pour grignotter!
Le programme avec les détails!
Du vin! De l'eau! Des cigarettes!
A deux cuartos! A deux cuartos! etc.
Yoyez! A deux cuartos!
Señoras et caballeros!

ZUNIGA
Des oranges, vite!

PLUSIEURS MARCHANDS

running up

En voici,
prenez, prenez, mesdemoiselles.

CHORUS
Two cuartos! Two cuartos!
Fans to cool yourselves!
Oranges to nibble!
Programme with details!
Wine! Water! Cigarettes!
Two cuartos! Two cuartos! etc.
Look! For two cuartos!
Señoras and caballeros!

ZUNIGA
Some oranges, look sharp!

SEVERAL FRUITSELLERS

Here you are,
take these, ladies.

Un Marchand	**One of Them**

to Zuniga, who pays

Merci, mon officier, merci.	Thank you, officer, thank you.

Les Autres Marchands	**The Others**
Celles-ci, Señor, sont plus belles.	These ones her, sir, are better.
Des éventails pour s'éventer, etc.	Fans to cool yourselves, etc.

Zuniga	**Zuniga**
Holà! des éventails!	Here you! Some fans!

Un Bohémien	**A Gypsy**

running forward

Voulez-vous aussi des lorgnettes?	Want some opera glasses too?

disc no. 2/track 15 *À deux cuartos!* The opening chorus of Act IV is one of the most exciting moments in opera, as the crowd gathers for the toreador's procession before the bullfight. Finally, after a brief introduction, we hear the principal theme that is introduced in the opera's prelude **(02:46)**, as the chorus sings in counterpoint, hailing the spectacle that comes to a grand conclusion at the arrival of Escamillo with Carmen on his arm.

A SCENE FROM THE FINAL ACT IN A PRODUCTION STAGED BY THE SAN DIEGO OPERA.

REPRISE DU CHOEUR
A deux cuartos! A deux cuartos!
Voyez! voyez! A deux cuartos! etc.

ZUNIGA
Qu'avez-vous donc fait de la Carmencita?

FRASQUITA
Escamillo est ici, la Carmencita ne doit pas
être loin.

ZUNIGA
Ah! c'est Escamillo, maintenant?

FRASQUITA
Et son ancien amoureux José, qu'est-il
devenu?

MERCÉDÈS
Il est libre.

ZUNIGA
Pour le moment.

FRASQUITA
Je ne serais pas tranquille à la place de
Carmen, je ne serais pas tranquille du tout.

CHORUS *(reprise)*
Two cuartos! Two cuartos!
Look! Look! Two cuartos! etc.

ZUNIGA
But what have you done with Carmencita?

FRASQUITA
Escamillo is here, Carmencita can't be far
off.

ZUNIGA
Ah! It's Escamillo now?

FRASQUITA
And her former lover Don José, what's
become of him?

MERCÉDÈS
He's at large.

ZUNIGA
For the moment.

FRASQUITA
I shouldn't feel easy in Carmen's place,
I shouldn't feel easy at all.

From outside loud shuts are heard, trumpet calls, etc. The Cuadrilla is arriving.

Scene Twenty-five **CHORUS AND SCENE**

CHOEUR
Les voici! Voici la quadrille!
La quadrille des toréros!
Sur les lances le soleil brille!

CHORUS
Here they come! Here's the cuadrilla!
The toreadors' cuadrilla!
The sun flashes on their lances!

En l'air toques et sombreros!
Les voici! voici la quadrille,
la quadrille des toréros!
Voici, débouchant sur la place,
voici d'abord, marchant au pas,
l'alguazil à vilaine face!
A bas! à bas! à bas! à bas!
Et puis saluons au passage,
saluons les hardis chulos!
Bravo! viva! gloire au courage!
Voici les hardis chulos!
Voyez les banderilleros!
Voyez quel air de crânerie!
Voyez! voyez! voyez! voyez!
Quel regards, et de quel éclat
étincelle la broderie
de leur costume de combat!
Voici les banderilleros!
Un autre quadrille s'avance!
Voyez les picadors!
Comm ils sont beaux!
Comme ils vont du fer de leur lance,
harceler le flanc des taureaux!

Up in the air with your caps and hats!
Here they are! Here's the cuadrilla,
the toreadors' cuadrilla!
Here, coming into the square
first of all, marching on foot,
is the constable with his ugly mug!
Down with him! Down with him!
And now as they go by
let's cheer the bold *chulos*!
Bravo! Hurrah! Glory to courage!
Here come the bold *chulos*!
Look at the *banderilleros*!
See what a swaggering air!
See them! See them!
What looks, and how brilliantly
the ornaments glitter
on their fighting dress!
Here are the banderilleros!
Another cuadrilla's coming!
Look at the *picadors*!
How handsome they are!
How they'll torment the bull's flanks
with the tips of their lances!

At last Escamillo appears, accompanied by a radiant and magnificently dressed Carmen.

L'Espada! Escamillo!
C'est l'Espada, la fine lame,
celui qui vient terminer tout,
qui paraît à la fin du drame
et qui frappe le dernier coup!
Vive Escamillo! ah bravo!
Les voici! Voici la quadrille! etc.

The Matador! Escamillo!
It's the Matador, the skilled swordsman,
he who comes to finish things off,
who appears at the drama's end
and strikes the last blow!
Long live Escamillo! Ah bravo!
Here they are! Here's the cuadrilla! etc.

ESCAMILLO *(à Carmen)*
Si tu m'aimes, Carmen, tu pourras, tout à

ESCAMILLO *(to Carmen)*
If you love me, Carmen, soon

l'heure,
être fière de moi.

CARMEN
Ah! je t'aime, Escamillo, je t'aime,
et que je meure si j'ai jamais aimé
quelqu'un autant que toi!

TOUS LES DEUX
Ah! je t'aime!
Oui, je t'aime!

LES ALGUAZILS
Place, place! place au seigneur Alcade!

CARMEN
Ah! I love you, Escamillo, I love you,
and may I die if I have ever loved
anyone as much as you!

TOGETHER
Ah! I love you!
Yes, I love you!

ALGUAZILS
Make way! Make way for his worship the
Mayor!

During a little orchestral march the Mayor enters and crosses the stage, preceded and followed by an escort of constables. Meanwhile Frasquita and Mercédès draw near to Carmen.

FRASQUITA
Carmen, un bon conseil, ne reste pas ici!

CARMEN
Et pourquoi, s'il te plaît?

MERCÉDÈS
Il est là!

CARMEN
Qui donc?

MERCÉDÈS
Lui, Don José!
Dans la foule il se cache; regarde.

FRASQUITA
Carmen, a word of advice, don't stay here!

CARMEN
And why, if you please?

MERCÉDÈS
He's there!

CARMEN
Who?

MERCÉDÈS
Him, Don José!
He's hiding among the crowd; look.

CARMEN
Oui, je le vois.

FRASQUITA
Prends garde!

CARMEN
Je ne suis pas femme à trembler devant lui.
Je l'attends, et je vais lui parler.

MERCÉDÈS
Carmen, crois-moi, prends garde!

CARMEN
Je ne crains rien!

FRASQUITA
Prends garde!

CARMEN
Yes, I see him.

FRASQUITA
Take care!

CARMEN
I'm not a woman to tremble in front of him.
I'm expecting him, and I'll speak to him.

MERCÉDÈS
Carmen, believe me, take care!

CARMEN
I'm not afraid of anything!

FRASQUITA
Take care!

*The mayor's cortège has entered the arena. Behind him, the procession of the
cuadrilla resumes its march and goes into the ring. The crowd follows . . . and in
withdrawing has revealed Don José, leaving him and Carmen alone downstage.*

Scene Twenty-six **DUET AND FINAL CHORUS**

disc no. 2/track 16 *C'est toi! C'est moi!* The spectacular opening brings the listener to the
greatest pages in the entire score, the final confrontation between Don José and
Carmen. The fugitive Don José emerges from the shadows as the magnificently
dressed Carmen, barely surprised, awaits her destiny. He is pitiful, crying to her
in sobbing phrases **(00:55)** that he wants another chance to love her. She dismisses him coldly, which only makes him beg more fervently. The melody that
he sings to the words "Carmen, il est temps encore" **(01:50)** reveals the depth
of his agony, but Carmen sings the same melody back to him as she denies
him, even in the face of death. When Don José realizes that she means what
she is saying **(03:47)**, he makes one last desperate attempt to convince her.

CARMEN
C'est toi!

JOSÉ
C'est moi!

CARMEN
L'on m'avait avertie
que tu n'étais pas loin, que tu devais venir;
l'on m'avait même dit de craindre pour ma vie
mais je suis brave et n'ai pas voulu fuir.

JOSÉ
Je ne menace pas, j'implore, je supplie;
notre passé, Carmen, je l'oublie.
Oui, nous allons tous deux
commencer une autre vie,
loin d'ici, sous d'autres cieux!

CARMEN
Tu demandes l'impossible,
Carmen jamais n'a menti;
son âme reste inflexible.
Entre elle et toi, tout est fini.
Jamais je n'ai menti;
entre nous, tout est fini.

JOSÉ
Carmen, il est temps encore,
oui, il est temps encore.
O ma Carmen, laisse-moi
te sauver, toi que j'adore,
et me sauver avec toi!

CARMEN
It's you!

JOSÉ
Yes, me!

CARMEN
I'd been warned
that you were about, that you might come here;
I was even told to fear for my life,
but I'm no coward and had no intention of running away.

JOSÉ
I'm not threatening, I'm imploring,
beseeching; our past, Carmen,—I forget it!
Yes, together we are going to begin
another life,
far from here, under new skies!

CARMEN
You ask the impossible,
Carmen has never lied;
her mind is made up.
Between her and you everything's finished.
I have never lied;
all's over between us.

JOSÉ
Carmen, there is still time,
yes, there is still time.
O my Carmen, let me
save you, you I adore,
and save myself with you!

CARMEN

Non, je sais bien que c'est l'heure
je sais bien que tu me tueras;
mais que je vive ou que je meure,
non, non, je ne tu céderai pas!

JOSÉ

Carmen, il est temps encor.
Ô ma Carmen, laisse-moi
te sauver, toi que j'adore;
ah! laisse-moi te sauver
et me sauver avec toi!
O ma Carmen, il est temps encore, etc.

CARMEN

Pourquoi t'occuper encore
d'un coeur qui n'est plus à toi?
Non, ce coeur n'est plus à toi!
En vain tu dis "Je t'adore",
tu n'obtiendras rien, non, rien de moi.
Ah! c'est en vain,
tu n'obtiendras rien, rien de moi!

JOSÉ

Tu ne m'aimes donc plus?

Carmen is silent.

Tu ne m'aimes donc plus?

CARMEN

Non, je ne t'aime plus.

JOSÉ

Mais moi, Carmen, je t'aime encore;
Carmen, hélas! moi, je t'adore!

CARMEN

No, I'm well aware that the hour has come,
I know that you are going to kill me;
but whether I live or die,
no, no, I shall not give in to you!

JOSÉ

Carmen, there is still time,
O my Carmen, let me
save you, you whom I adore;
ah! let me save you
and save myself with you!
O my Carmen, there is still time, etc.

CARMEN

Why still concern yourself
with a heart that's no longer yours?
No, this heart no longer belongs to you!
In vain you say "I adore you,"
you'll get nothing, no nothing, from me.
Ah! It's useless,
you'll get nothing, nothing, from me!

JOSÉ

Then you don't love me any more?

Then you don't love me any more?

CARMEN

No, I don't love you any more.

JOSÉ

But I, Carmen, I love you still;
Carmen, alas! I adore you!

CARMEN
A quoi bon tout cela? que mots superflus!

JOSÉ
Carmen, je t'aime, je t'adore!
Eh bien, s'il le faut, pour te plaire,
je resterai bandit, tout ce que tu voudras—
tout, tu m'entends? Tout!
Mais ne me quitte pas,
ô ma Carmen,
ah! souviens-toi, souviens-toi du passé!
Nous nous aimions naguère!
Ah! ne me quitte pas, Carmen,
ah, ne me quitte pas!

CARMEN
Jamais Carmen ne cédera!
Libre elle est née et libre elle mourra!

CHŒUR ET FANFARES *(dans le cirque)*
Viva! viva! la course est belle!
Viva! sur le sable sanglant
le taureau, le taureau s'élance!
Voyez! voyez! voyez!
Le taureau qu'on harcèle
en bondissant s'élance, voyez!
Frappé juste, en plein coeur,
voyez! voyez! voyez!
Victoire!

CARMEN
What's the good of this? What waste of
words!

JOSÉ
Carmen, I love you, I adore you!
All right, if I must, to please you
I'll stay a bandit, anything you like—
anything, do you hear? Anything!
But do not leave me,
O my Carmen,
ah! remember the past!
We loved each other once!
Ah! do not leave me, Carmen,
ah, do not leave me!

CARMEN
Carmen will never yield!
Free she was born and free she will die!

CHORUS AND FANFARES *(in the arena)*
Hurrah! Hurrah! A grand fight!
Hurrah! Across the bloodstained sand
the bull charges!
Look! Look! Look!
The tormented bull
comes bounding to the attack, look!
Struck true, right to the heart,
Look! Look! Look!
Victory!

During the chorus, Carmen and José remain silent, both listening. Hearing shouts of "Victory!" a cry of delight escapes Carmen. Don José's eyes are fixed upon her. The chorus over, she takes a step towards the main entrance of the ring.

disc no. 2/track 17 *Où vas-tu?* Don José quickly unravels, and the music dizzily and sickeningly reflects the quick, violent action that follows when Carmen tries to escape and go to Escamillo, whose triumph echoes from the arena. The confrontation turns ugly and vicious—Carmen insults Don José with a derisive shout of "Tiens!" (There!) **(01:50)** when she throws the ring he gave her in his face. Unafraid, she strides confidently toward the arena (0158) and an enraged Don José steps forward and stabs her to death. As she falls lifeless to the ground—the fate motive triumphant at last in the orchestra **(02:22)**—he weeps over her, singing of his love as the opera ends on a grim final chord.

THE FINAL CONFRONTATION BETWEEN CARMEN AND DON JOSÉ IN A PRODUCTION AT THE METROPOLITAN OPERA.

JOSÉ

blocking her way

Où vas-tu?

CARMEN
Laisse-moi!

JOSÉ

Where are you going?

CARMEN
Leave me alone!

JOSÉ
Cet homme qu'on acclame,
c'est ton nouvel amant!

CARMEN
Laisse-moi! Laisse-moi!

JOSÉ
Sur mon âme,
tu ne passeras pas,
Carmen, c'est moi que tu suivras!

CARMEN
Laisse-moi, Don José, je ne te suivrai pas.

JOSÉ
Tu vas le retrouver. Dis . . . tu l'aimes
donc?

CARMEN
Je l'aime!
Je l'aime, et devant la mort même,
je répéterais que je l'aime!

JOSÉ
This man they're cheering,
he's your new lover!

CARMEN
Leave me alone! Leave me alone!

JOSÉ
By my soul,
you won't get past,
Carmen, you will come with me!

CARMEN
Let me go, Don José, I'm not going with you.

JOSÉ
You're going to him. Tell me . . . you love
him then?

CARMEN
I love him!
I love him, and in the face of death itself
I would go on saying I love him!

shouts and fanfares again from the arena

CHOEUR
Viva! La course est belle! etc.

JOSÉ
Ainsi, le salut de mon âme,
je l'aurai perdu pour que toi,
pour que tu t'en ailles, infâme,
entre ses bras, rire de moi!
Non, par le sang, tu n'irais pas!
Carmen, c'est moi que tu suivras!

CHORUS
Hurrah! A grand fight! etc.

JOSÉ
So I am to lose
my heart's salvation so that you
can run to him, infamous creature,
to laugh at me in his arms!
No, by my blood, you shall not go!
Carmen, you're coming with me!

CARMEN
Non! non! jamais!

JOSÉ
Je suis las de te menacer!

CARMEN
Eh bien! Frappe-moi donc, ou laisse-moi
passer!

CHŒUR
Victoire!

JOSÉ
Pour la dernière fois, démon,
veux-tu me suivre?

CARMEN
Non! non!
Cette bague autrefois,
tu me l'avais donnée,
tiens!

She throws it away.

JOSÉ

advancing on Carmen, knife in hand

Eh bien, damnée!

Carmen draws back, José following, as fanfares sound again in the ring.

CHŒUR
Toréador, en guarde!
Et songe bien, oui, songe en combattant,

CARMEN
No! No! Never!

JOSÉ
I'm tired of threatening you!

CARMEN
All right, stab me then, or let me pass!

CHORUS
Victory!

JOSÉ
For the last time, you devil,
will you come with me?

CARMEN
No! No!
This ring that you
once gave me—
here, take it!

JOSÉ

All right, accursed woman!

CHORUS
Toreador, on guard!
And remember, yes, remember as you fight

qu'un oeil noir te regarde,
et que l'amour t'attend!

that two dark eyes are watching you,
and that love awaits you!

Don José stabs Carmen; she falls dead. The curtains are thrown open and the crowd comes out of the arena.

JOSÉ
Vous pouvez m'arrêter.
C'est moi qui l'ai tuée.

JOSÉ
You can arrest me.
I was the one who killed her!

Escamillo appears on the arena steps. Don José throws himself upon Carmen's body.

Ah! Carmen! ma Carmen adorée!

Ah! Carmen! My adored Carmen!

THE END

Carmen

GEORGES BIZET

LIBRETTO BY MEILHAC & HALEVY

COMPACT DISC ONE

Deuxieme Acte/Act Two

COMPACT DISC TWO

Troisième Acte/Act Three

6   Écoute, écoute   4:00
    Choeur/Dancaire/Remendado/José/Carmen/Mercedes/Frasquita

7   Reposons-nous une heure ici, mes camarades   1:00
    Dancaire/Remendado/José/Carmen

8   A la bonne heure . . . Mêlons! Coupons! *(Card Trio)*   7:04
    Carmen/José/Frasquita/Mercédès

9   Eh bien?   3:34
    Carmen/Dancaïre/José/Mercédès/Frasquita/Choeur

10   Quante au douanier, c'est notre affaire   0:43

11   Oui, je reste! . . . Je dis que rien ne m'épouvante   5:44
    Le Guide/Micaëla

12   Mais . . je ne me trompe pas   5:57
    Micaëla/Escamillo/José

13   Holâ, Holâ! José!   8:41
    Carmen/Escamillo/Dancaïre/José/Micaëla/Frasquita/
    Mercedes/Remendado/Choeur

14   Entre'acte *(Orchestre)*   2:13

Quatrieme Acte/Act Four

15   A deux cuartes!   9:02
    Choeur/Zuniga/Plusieurs Marchands/In Bohèmien

16   C'est toi! C'est moi!   6:02

17   Où vas-tu?   3:31